THE
PRINCIPLES
OF
PHILOSOPHY

THE PRINCIPLES OF PHILOSOPHY

MICHAEL MOORE

SIRIUS

SIRIUS

This edition published in 2023 by Sirius Publishing, a division of
Arcturus Publishing Limited,
26/27 Bickels Yard, 151–153 Bermondsey Street,
London SE1 3HA

ISBN: 978-1-3988-3007-3
AD010136UK

Printed in China

CONTENTS

INTRODUCTION

What is Philosophy?

The practice of philosophy is something society performs upon itself, a form of sophisticated self-awareness in which we try to understand ourselves and the world around us. There can be a temptation to see philosophy as primarily about giving voice to insights one has already arrived at, almost as if the real goal is to announce to the world the wisdom it has long missed.

But the greater part of philosophy concerns the investigation and exploration of every part of life.

Among the early Greeks, who were the first Western philosophers, many thinkers turned their attention to the physical world, and this curiosity of investigation eventually spread out into diverse areas of human activity such as ethics, literature, beauty, and just about anything else you could think of. While much of the discipline of philosophy is taken up with analysing and pursuing questions, it would not be quite right to say that it does not have answers, or does not make progress – consider the use of formal logic in many electronic applications, for example, or how the fields of biology and physics, to name just two instances, found their origin in philosophy before becoming the independent sciences they are today.

The horizons of philosophy, much like those of humanity in general, are always expanding. There are new areas to investigate prompted by new human endeavours, such as the ethics of online privacy or artificial intelligence. Likewise there are fads of current interest and dynamic controversies introduced by cutting-edge philosophers. In the 20th century much interest in anglophone philosophy turned to analysing language itself, translating language into mathematical statements, clarifying what language is and how it works, and attempting to identify the more treacherous ways that language can deceive us at a conceptual level.

Changes which have been occurring for decades at the academic level have continued apace, with philosophy tending toward specialization and scholarship more than polymathy and innovation. One unfortunate result is that many professional philosophers do not have a grounding in the history of their field. There are, of course, many things to know and many philosophers to learn about in the history of philosophy.

One way to approach the study of philosophy is to focus on the high points, those influential ideas and figures which not only made an impact at the time, but directly influence other thinkers even up to the current time. Though any such survey is bound to skip over some elements while playing up others, this present book covers ten of the most consequential subfields within philosophy itself. Nature, Knowledge, Metaphysics, Logic, Ethics, Language, Mind, Aesthetics, Politics and Religion contain a wealth of philosophical knowledge. While some of these subjects, such as knowledge, might be considered more

The Ancient Greeks were the first known Western philosophers.

stereotypically philosophical, whereas others – for instance religion – are not, we should note that philosophy is an analytical tool that can be applied to any field.

In proceeding through the chapters it will become quite evident that different parts of philosophy share ambiguous boundaries with one another. What seems like a question of logic may also be considered a problem for language. A metaphysical paradox really invokes deep religious concerns as well. Philosophy is something that twists and turns its way into every avenue of human activity, and to try to separate things discretely is only to immerse a question into other philosophical issues as well.

How to use this book

This book is meant to provide an overview of ten different fields of philosophy. The overview centres on the idea of 'principles' and what is in mind are the central ideas and important pillars within the given field of philosophy. Within each chapter this is an intellectual task mostly split between the sections 'History of Philosophy', usually related through singular philosophers making significant contributions, and 'Important Principles', a section which isolates ideas important in their own right, whose details and influence merit special attention.

Each chapter also includes a section of questions, which are intended both to motivate the discussion to follow and to provoke further consideration of the chapter's themes – but there need be no expectation of ironclad answers. Near the end of each chapter comes a section on 'Principles of X and You', intended to either make practical connections with the philosophical content or clarify the findings of the chapter. Finally there is a list of summary points, to capture in brief the discussion of the chapter in a memorable way.

Some concepts are quite intuitive, such as the distinction between token and type; when you gain an appreciation for how to apply these labels, they can prove a very effective conceptual tool for thinking. But other ideas in this book, such as the abstract discussion about universals, are very difficult to think through. The intention is not to give you an exhaustive handle on the concept, but rather to provide a general glimpse, such that it will spur you to further reading on the topic or at least give you an adequate outline.

Unlike other casual reading material, such as a newspaper article or a beach novel, philosophical reading often requires pausing and reflection. The ideas are sometimes new or strange to our way of thinking and take a bit of digestion before proceeding. Working one's way through the material slowly is to be desired. As mentioned, there are questions at the beginning of each chapter. Using these or coming up with your own questions for the chapter topic will help as you read through the chapter. Asking a question is a natural way to stoke the philosophical spirit through our personal curiosity.

I hope you will find this book useful as an overview of these topics, a spur to further reading, an expansion of the scope of philosophical enquiry and stimulation for your own intellectual journey.

Philosophy contains a range of different subjects and the ideas within can provide insights in every field of human knowledge.

THE PRINCIPLES OF NATURE

What is nature? This is not as easy to answer as it may first appear. Our first inclination is probably to think of nature either in the context of human nature or in terms of the great outdoors – a garden, park, forest or beach. Following this approach, we would distinguish the realm of nature primarily as the features of the world which are not in any way manmade constructs.

Nature is so familiar to us that we seldom think about it. We take it for granted that nature exists, and that it evidences an order which we can understand. But how do we come to understand nature? Before we reach a satisfying definition, it would be helpful if we could determine some rules or guidelines about how nature works: the principles of nature.

A principle of nature is straightforwardly a way to account for how nature 'works', in the broadest sense. In modern parlance it often takes the form of a declarative sentence. It can apply to anything from nature as a whole to galaxies, animals or individual atoms, via biology, chemistry, physics and anything in between. 'Light always travels in a straight line' and 'When one object exerts force on a second object, the second object exerts an equal and opposite force back on the first' are two clear examples of such declarative sentences in relation to nature. These formulations are frequently encountered in science books in a classroom, but are equally often put into mathematical terms to express the law as precisely as possible. Although we are most familiar with such mathematical or sentential forms of principles, the earliest principles of nature, from early Greek philosophy, were expressed in the form of a primary driving force, with all it involved – a single element, like fire or water, or sometimes more than one element, like love and strife.

Questions on Nature

One of the primordial questions in philosophy concerns the nature of reality, where we understand 'reality' to be nearly synonymous with 'world' or 'universe'. We wish to know what the world around us really is. If we ask, 'What is the "nature" of the world or universe?' we expect that the answer we find will enable us to come to know in a fundamental way what our world is really about. We are attempting to move from more specific pieces of information about nature to a more overarching understanding of the concept. The 'principles of nature' (or more familiarly the 'laws of nature') are really about helping us identify what nature is by telling us how nature works. There is a natural progression from 'What is the universe?' to 'What is the nature of the universe?' to 'How does nature work?' to 'What are the principles of nature?'. When we get a grasp of the particulars, as seen in laws and principles, this will fill in our knowledge of what nature is as a whole.

The great outdoors – how we tend to think of nature.

A Brief History of the Philosophy of Nature

Nature is all around us. This presents two difficulties. Its familiarity can cause problems in that it can be hard to separate ourselves from nature enough to understand it. A second and more serious point is that the concept of nature applies, by definition, to everything in our universe. So whatever we are going to say about nature will be broad, as the scope of our description must capture broad truths and general applications. This is not to say that the search for the principles of nature is divorced from the real world. As we will see, the investigation historically began with the physical world.

An additional idea to keep in mind is that the way we conceive of nature determines the way we approach our study of it. For instance, when the role of females in society was exclusively as mothers, nature was viewed as feminine in light of this same kind of generative power. As a consequence of the belief that nature is feminine, the search for the principles of nature has sometimes reflected the manner in which men interacted with and pursued women. One way this influenced the study of nature was that nature was seen as coy, and so knowledge must be coaxed out of her. There has also been an impulse to control nature – in the sense that gaining a knowledge of the principles of nature confers a power over it, analogous to the way in previous times men were thought to rule over women. Francis Bacon, the 17th-century philosopher and scientist, captures this idea well with the maxim 'Knowledge is power'. For Bacon, having control and power over nature is the real knowledge of nature we should pursue.

The Greeks and the First Principles

The ancient Greeks were the first to pursue principles in this way, embarking on their search in the context of nature, from about 500 BCE. The aim of these philosophers was not merely to satisfy their curiosity, but was a search for explanation of the physical phenomena in the world: an explanation of where the world comes from, how it comes to be, and what this can tell us about the nature of human beings who live in such an environment.

In the image, text appears within the painting:

Sᵣ Francis Bacon, Lord
Keeper and afterwards
Lord Chancellor of
England, 1617

Francis Bacon.

Anaximenes.

HISTORICAL PRINCIPLES OF NATURE	
PRINCIPLE	PHILOSOPHER
WATER	THALES
AIR	ANAXIMENES
FIRE	HERACLITUS
ATOMS	DEMOCRITUS
LOVE AND STRIFE	EMPEDOCLES

In the context of attempting to explain the physical phenomena around us, principles were and are fundamental. This capacity to explain goes a long way in establishing the usefulness of principles. Both historians and philosophers distinguish these early Greek attempts at finding physical principles from the primarily mythological method of interpreting the world common at the time. Whatever else philosophy may be, a central aspiration of its method is to find explanations and causes. One philosopher, Anaximenes, posited air as the principle for the universe, while another, Anaximander, said that everything came from what he termed the 'unlimited'. Sitting as we are in a position of historical evaluation, it is quite easy to dismiss such principles as fanciful speculation. But we would be missing the subtlety and consistency of these philosophical pioneers if we so readily dismissed their principles as nothing more than ignorant and arbitrary stabs in the dark. Anaximenes, for instance, in positing air as the singular principle of the universe, probably realized that whatever created and sustained the world must itself be in motion, in order to convey motion to the rest of the world. Air, itself invisible, seems like a good candidate to be taking care of things behind the scenes because it seems to be present everywhere. Whatever we think is responsible for the physical makeup of the universe determines how we think of the universe. If we think that the world is fundamentally made up of air, then suddenly the speed of wind along with its temperature, duration and direction will take on great importance.

Aristotle on Nature

The great philosopher Aristotle (384–322 BCE) characterized nature, among other things, as the processes of change. Things come into existence and pass away, in life and death, and there are also less dramatic instances of change, such as coming to be bigger or smaller, as when a baby turns into a child, or change of colour, for example, when a green leaf turns red in the autumn. For Aristotle this was the study of 'physics', a term which comes from the Greek word for nature. Calling the study of nature 'physics' has persisted in Western civilization even up to the present.

The Greek search for principles was a necessary first step in the development of the scientific method which was to become so common in the West. However, this initial investigation aimed only at finding a physical first cause – some material substance or object which created the universe or which all the universe was made out of. If you look at an elaborate diorama of a city made out of Lego building blocks, these rectangular pieces of plastic would be the first principle, in the Greek sense, of this play city. Likewise, the software on a computer, despite one program being a spreadsheet and another a video game, is all made out of computer code. Thus the first principle of a computer is code.

Lego building blocks are the principles of a lego city.

Looking at this early history of Greek philosophy, we see that these first principles were centred primarily on common natural substances, like water or fire, as the explanations for the makeup of the universe. But with the introduction of the idea of a principle, principles themselves began to change, to take on a new and broader meaning beyond the merely physical.

Principles as Order

If we take a step back for a moment, the search for the principles of nature can be characterized as a search for order. Yet, such principles are unsatisfying even if properly identified. One may ask, 'Well, why do I care if fire or ether or something else accounts for the ultimate structure of the universe?' Following a common pattern with philosophical words, the idea of a 'principle' began to expand and change. In this new sense, principles became more abstract, partly because they were being invoked to explain a broad range of phenomena, and partly because they arose from repeated observation and experience, not any single instance. At any rate the meaning of the principles of nature began to be understood in a more law-like fashion.

Stoics and Law-like Principles

While in one sense there was a shift in the meaning of 'principle', so that the term gained an additional force, another group of philosophers, the Stoics, coming along shortly after Aristotle, helped to blur the line of distinction between principle as a material origin and principle as a law. The Stoic outlook took very seriously the idea of living 'in accordance with nature'. This meant not only determining what the normal ways of nature were but also acknowledging that these laws of nature make a claim on how we ourselves are to live. How we ought to live is a reflection of how the world exists in fact.

Principles as Laws

We are so familiar with the term 'law of nature' that the impact of the phrase has escaped our notice. But to call something a law of nature is to invoke a comparison between human laws and these so-called laws of nature. In fact, one of the distinguishing features of laws of nature is that they cannot be broken. This contrasts sharply with human laws, which are broken all the time. What we can take away from this is that laws of nature, as principles, are the exemplary cases of order in the world we inhabit. Never too far from this discussion is the role of God, who is the presumed originator of these laws, whether

Robert Boyle.

as the traditional god of monotheism or the divine-like demiurge of Plato, fashioning the world after an eternal model, or Zeus, the logical creator and sustainer.

One of the first significant disagreements on this issue centred on whether the study of nature was to be conducted through theoretical consideration or empirical observation. Due in large part to the influence of classical Greek philosophy, even up through the Middle Ages, loyalty to Aristotle's intricate physical system pushed scientific endeavours away from more empirically based experimentation and observation in favour of self-standing theoretical consistency.

Nature as a Mechanism Following Laws

In the 16th century, scientists such as Galileo and Francis Bacon began to steer scientific investigation towards the empirically testable and experimentally verified. In 1686, Robert Boyle, often considered the founder of modern chemistry, wrote a treatise, *Free Enquiry into the Vulgarly Receiv'd Notion of Nature*. What is notable about this book is that it argued we should not personify Nature into someone who pursues noble goals such as 'Nature does nothing in vain' or 'Nature abhors a vacuum'. Rather nature works mechanically, and for this reason is to be understood in terms of a consistent predictability discoverable by human investigation. This was a key movement in the history of understanding the laws of nature as principles, since it placed a renewed emphasis upon human investigation.

THE NATURE OF A HUMAN COMPARED TO A MACHINE IS DRASTICALLY DIFFERENT

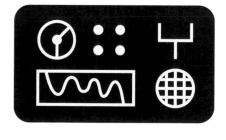

VS

Person

Machine

The Principles of Nature Are Beyond Human Knowledge

In his *Essay Concerning Human Understanding* (1690) John Locke took this idea of the regularity of nature to what he understood as its logical, perhaps extreme, conclusion. His insight was that if we knew the shapes and activities of atoms and the ways in which atomic shapes and activities affected other bodies, then in theory we could know how everything in the world operates or moves. This would be the only foolproof method of scientific knowledge. But such a knowledge of the behaviour and other qualities of atoms is in fact wholly beyond the scope of human abilities. Humans are ignorant of the true reality of the principles of nature. What we have as a makeshift substitute are generalizations about nature which seem to be true based on the information we have gathered from our limited and fallible experience.

Earlier we discussed the importance of order in forming an understanding of the principles of nature. On Locke's conception we have to concede that our knowledge limits our access to these principles. We have to make do with approximations of them which may not hold true in every case.

Whether principles do hold true in every case has been a contentious issue, deeply involved with the question of whether we can ever come to know, or be justified in believing, that what we deem 'principles' are in fact principles. Principles are generalizations, universalizations, which eliminate exceptions and give us a clear, ironclad rule to apply to the world. Newton's first law of motion (published in 1687), for example – 'A body remains at rest until it is acted upon by a force' – is true at all times and all places, and is a totalizing generalization, or at least it claims to be. Disputes over what constitutes a principle would shape much thinking on the subject that followed.

Explanation vs Unification

In the early 20th century Carl Hempel and Paul Oppenheim developed a view about science which relied on explanation. Their idea was that explanation, first and foremost, should be the guiding concern for formulating laws or principles about nature. They called such an explanation 'a covering law of explanation', and by this they meant that the law covered or explained all the cases under investigation. Under the concept of a covering law, the explanation must be able to be put into the form of a logical argument, with premises and a conclusion. A covering law also had to include a law of nature, so that the law could account for whatever phenomena were being considered. Along with its formalism, one of the benefits of the covering law was that it clearly predicted how future instances of the same law would come about. Prediction is related directly to explanation: if some natural event can be explained, then instances of the same kind can be predicted when the same circumstances arise again.

The hardest cases for covering laws to account for are patterns, as opposed to specific events or circumstances. The reason is that patterns often are not exact, but are irregular and inconsistent, despite the general tendency towards design. It is difficult to formulate a law which has a number of exceptions, especially when those exceptions are embedded in a complicated pattern.

These and other problems eventually led to the general abandonment of covering laws as an explanation. One alternative was the unificationist approach to natural phenomena. This theory moved away from laws to more general principles. In effect this amounts to proposing fewer things. Through attempting to gather all phenomena and

A COVERING LAW ACCOUNTS FOR ALL INSTANCES

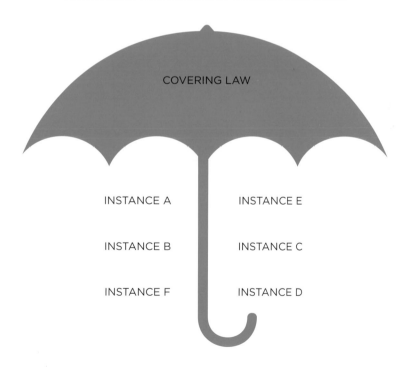

COVERING LAW

INSTANCE A INSTANCE E

INSTANCE B INSTANCE C

INSTANCE F INSTANCE D

data under a single heading, the general theory unifies all the details of the particulars. It should be noted that this unificationist project was undertaken as an acknowledgement of the failure of the covering law theory. Thus, unificationist theory does not seek out causes, but appeals to a process of simplification as its explanation.

We have seen throughout this discussion of the principles and laws of nature that there is almost an inescapable focus on cause and effect (see also section on Cause and Effect, in Important Principles below) although some philosophers have attempted to abandon this reliance on causation. When we have invoked the idea of principles, what we are doing is tying one phenomenon, or fact, to another. So when water reaches zero degrees Celsius, the principle, if we were to formulate it, would be something like 'When

Freezing water.

water becomes 32 degrees Celsius or colder it freezes'. There is a connection between the temperature of water and its freezing or not doing so. Because the freezing is linked to the temperature of the water, we believe the temperature, in some sense, is the cause of the freezing of the water. The law or temperature can be said to 'dictate' the results of what happens, and the phenomena can be said to 'obey' the law. This superintendence means that the 'direction' goes from cause to effect, but not vice versa.

Some have detected in the very idea of cause and effect a commitment to something beyond what can be confirmed by our eyes and other senses – what philosophers call 'metaphysics' (literally 'beyond physics'), an appeal to the realm of invisible (and perhaps ultimately unreachable) reality. For this reason they have shunned talk of causation, and do not look for relations of cause and effect, but for practical arrangements of phenomena. Such shyness about cause and effect has lead to alternative accounts of the regularity of nature, as seen above in unificationism or even in sceptical attacks on our assumptions about nature, such as we'll see in the criticism made by David Hume below. But now we are going to look at a different division in understanding the principles of nature.

Realism vs Anti-Realism

Realism is a commitment to a number of ideas about the role of science in interpreting the natural world around us. The most important of these is that the world we investigate has a real existence apart from what we see or think about it, and it is possible to

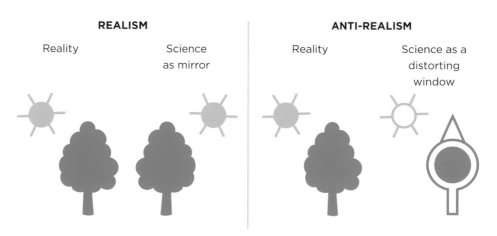

SCIENTIFIC REALISM VS ANTI-REALISM

REALISM | ANTI-REALISM

Reality | Science as mirror | Reality | Science as a distorting window accurately put into words the conclusions of our investigations into it (both for ourselves and for others). Uniting the separate elements of realism is the belief that the formal sciences 'really' represent knowledge about the natural universe.

Several objections to the realist position, under the heading of 'anti-realism', have been lodged. Most of these objections seek to poke sceptical holes in the ability of science or philosophy to give consistent or reliable answers about nature. Very commonly anti-realist arguments undermine faith that there are principles of nature, or bring into doubt that we could know or tell others about them.

The Pessimisitic Meta-Induction

The name sounds intimidating, but this is only longhand for a rather simple idea: an anti-realist argument aimed at undermining our trust in the laws and conclusions of science as we know them now (see also explanation of 'induction' in next section). History tells us that science is a developmental process; most theories and ideas have to be cast aside or altered in some degree to fit with new data and new ideas. It follows, according to the anti-realist, that the theories we possess now will likewise one day be shown obsolete because at least some part of them will be proved false.

There are two interesting aspects to this objection. The first is that the anti-realist acknowledges that the theories of science match up with the data, at least as well as they are able. So one apparent conclusion is that theories are not as precise as we think they are – if they were, they wouldn't be supplanted by new ones all the time. Perhaps more disturbing, however, is that even though any given current theory seems to match up with the phenomena, the meta-induction suggests this is because of the broad scope of the theory. So the geocentric model of the solar system explained astronomical observation well enough to even accommodate the apparent eccentricity of planetary motion, retrograde movements that, in our present hindsight, should have been red flags to ancient astronomers about the viability of their theory.

A second consequence of the meta-induction is that it suggests the formulas, laws or principles which we ascribe to nature are often imprecise, despite being crafted in such a way as to account for as many cases as possible. The conclusion for some anti-realists is that nature really doesn't have these principles, or that if they are to be found in nature, they are beyond the detectability of the human mind.

There are two general responses by the realists to the meta-induction. The first is to direct our attention to the progress which science has made over the centuries. Thus

Geocentric model of the solar system.

the idea is not that theories have given way to others at random, but that less precise theories have ceded to more precise (or less imprecise) theories. Science is moving toward capital-T 'Truth', even if slowly. Another appeal by the realists is to moderate the claim that science, strictly speaking, has possession of the truth. Rather science approximates the truth. This means that the laws or principles science arrives at resemble the truth to some degree, but just because they fall short of perfect fidelity does not mean that the realist position should be abandoned.

Important Principles of Nature

In this section we will discuss some of the principles that have been important to the study of nature by looking both at particular examples and at the different ways principles have been formulated. The first is what has often been termed the 'uniformity of nature'. This is the idea that the processes of the present continue on as they have in the past. Whatever causes and powers were at work one million or 20,000 years ago are still at play, and in the same way, today. By this principle of uniformity, for example, erosion can be estimated in the case of a mountain and, provided the rate of erosion from the elements has been similar to today, we can make a good estimate of what elevation it had in the year 1500.

When a principle is formed from this expectation of uniformity, this is called 'induction'. For example, imagine that we observe a number of white swans, one after

Mountain erosion.

another, and on every subsequent occasion we see a swan, it is also a white bird. We may come to the conclusion 'All swans are white' through this induction. The conclusion was arrived at through the expectation that all swans will be similar to our previous experience with other instances of the same bird.

A more modest form of a principle derived from induction is a principle from projection. The procedure is the same as that of induction, except that the conclusion is not extended to all swans, but a projection is made about the next swan we see: 'The next swan is projected to be white.'

One of the most popular varieties of induction in recent years has been the so-called 'inference to the best explanation', often shortened to 'IBE'. Suppose a toddler and a dog are left alone with a bag of wrapped chocolates. When you return you see a bunch of wrappers strewn on the ground. The dog and the toddler both stare at you innocently. When you inspect the remains of the sweets you see that there are what appear to be punctured holes in the wrappers and in assorted pieces of leftover chocolate. Your inference to the best explanation is that the dog's teeth were responsible for the chocolate thievery. Of course, someone else could claim that the child was savvy and used a toy screwdriver to get at the chocolate directly or, perhaps even with more sophistication, did so as a ploy to frame the dog while taking all the chocolate themself. This would not be the best inference, however – that distinction belongs to the theory that the dog ate the chocolate.

INFERENCE TO THE BEST EXPLANATION

| Baby | Dog with chocolate around its mouth | Chocolate bars with puncture marks |

WHAT IS THE BEST EXPLANATION?
A) THE DOG ATE THE CHOCOLATE
B) THE BABY ATE THE CHOCOLATE
C) THE BABY ATE THE CHOCOLATE AND FRAMED THE DOG

Hume and Induction

Perhaps due to the widespread acceptance of induction as a way of knowing the world, David Hume took aim in his work *A Treatise of Human Nature* (1739) at our casual acceptance of the uniformity of nature, attacking it with the 'problem of induction'. On this analysis, there are two possibilities as to where our knowledge of the world comes from: either 'relations of ideas' or 'matters of fact'. Knowledge that arises from 'relations of ideas' meets a very high standard, for it concerns either the certain knowledge of mathematics, geometry and algebra or any kind of knowledge that attains a comparable level of certainty. 'Relations of ideas' are reasoned about objects which are not perceivable or discoverable in the physical world. That is, 5 plus 5 equalling 10 is independent of the physical facts in the universe, and true even if there were never any universe at all. Likewise, the interior angles of a triangle add up to 180 degrees regardless of whether this shape is found anywhere in nature. 'Relations of ideas' concern ideas alone – they operate and their truth depends on the interaction of thoughts in the mind alone. One cannot deny them without entering into a contradiction. To say '2 and 2 is 5' is simply wrong.

On the other hand, 'matters of fact' are the kind of knowledge that we acquire only after experience and observation. Unlike 'relations of ideas' which are concepts only in the mind, matters of fact are observable in the world. Hume gives the example of the sunrise, and contrasts it with the logical propositions of maths, pointing out that denying the daily setting of the sun involves no logical contradiction, unlike denying that 10 times 10 is 100.

So how does Hume involve this analysis in his understanding of nature? Remember, he has said that all human reasoning concerns either relations of ideas or matter of fact, an either/or choice known as 'Hume's fork'. The events that occur in nature cannot be relations of ideas because they do not follow the mathematical certainty of relations of ideas, and unlike relations of ideas, events in nature are observable. This leaves matters of fact as the only alternative. It must be the case that what we observe of nature concerns matters of fact. However, this means that, contrary to what Hume's predecessors might have argued, there is no contradiction in the idea that the sun may not rise tomorrow. The sun may rise tomorrow or it may not, but whatever happens, there is no logical obstacle as to why one or the other will occur. Since there is nothing logically inconsistent in the sun failing to rise tomorrow, Hume said that we are not justified in taking past sunrises as evidence that there will be a future sunrise tomorrow.

Hume's objection to the assumption that the sun will rise tomorrow centred on the

David Hume.

way in which we arrived at the conclusion of regularity that we often assign to nature. The best justification we can muster for assuming the sun will rise tomorrow is that it not only rose today but on many other previous occasions in our personal experience. Yet there is no logical reason why it might not fail to rise tomorrow. This makes 'The sun rises each day' a different kind of proposition from the logically necessary '5 x 5 is 25' or 'Frozen water is ice'. It is not possible for frozen water to be anything other than ice but it is possible that the sun might not rise tomorrow. What Hume pointed out, among other things, is that it is difficult to justify our belief in principles unless we take for granted that past events are a surefire guide to the future.

Nature and Scientific Revolution

Nature is difficult to describe, and very often our efforts to formulate its principles come to nought. When our models of nature reach a crisis point and cannot account for past information or new data, or offer any promises of insight, then the possibility of a

Copernicus observing the night sky.

conceptual revolution arises. According to Thomas Kuhn in *The Structure of Scientific Revolutions* (1962), when the predominant scientific theory in a field fails to account for sufficient phenomena or is unable to innovate, a new paradigmatic theory that it is able to promise and deliver on the inabilities of the first theory will take over. In Kuhn's framing, scientific knowledge of the principles of nature proceeds through fits and starts as different theories are accepted and rejected. This is a more holistic understanding of the way in which principles of nature develop. Historically Kuhn is claiming that it is not individual principles which are collected here and there as they seem reasonable, but principles arise and are adopted to the degree that they fit within a broader scientific theory. He is saying, in other words, that principles are understood within a broader framework – a principle can only be understood within the context of a theory.

The relationship between the raw data of observational science and a given theory is that the theory shapes and formulates the data into a particular principle or principles. An interesting consequence of all this is that raw data alone is never sufficient by itself to determine a theory; rather a theory must be tentatively offered to explain the data, and this in turn means different competing theories could explain the same data. For example, two different sets of principles reflecting the orbit of the planets and the movements of stars can be offered by both a heliocentric and a geocentric view of the solar system. The geocentric principles, of course, will be more convoluted, but despite the liabilities geocentrism holds in other areas (including its falsity), it can explain the motion of the heavenly bodies even if the principles appear ad hoc when compared to a heliocentric model.

The 'Anything Goes' Model of Science

If Kuhn undermines our traditional confidence in the scientific method by showing how theories are constantly being overturned, then it should be no surprise that some philosophers have resorted to very radical methods in their study of science. One such figure was Paul Feyerabend. In his *Against Method* (1975) Feyerabend promoted the idea of 'epistemological anarchism'. A more colloquial expression of this same idea is 'anything goes'. He believed that, based on the history of science, progress is made when, figuratively speaking, a thousand flowers are free to bloom. Science is not a mechanical process with set rules which need to be followed. Rather, breakthroughs in science often come about through the insightful work of genius. In a very real way, science is much like art, and it must rely on the unrestricted creativity granted to art. Feyerabend made several compelling comparisons for why we should grant this anarchic freedom to science.

Broadly speaking, in his judgement, since we do not have a complete handle on the science we currently possess and we do not know what it will look like in the future, we have to be open to any possible tool at our disposal in order to make the progress required of science. From his standpoint, theoretical commitments are nothing but hindrances to scientific advancement.

Paul Feyerabend.

HOW SCIENTIFIC PROGRESS IS ACHIEVED

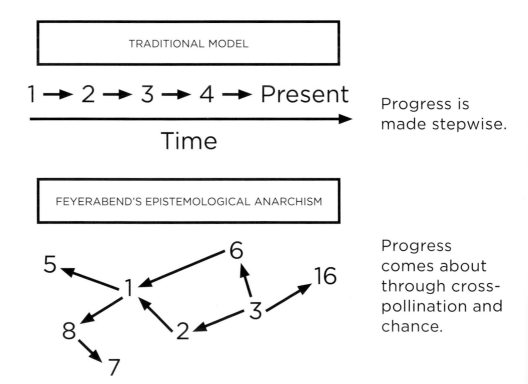

TRADITIONAL MODEL

$1 \rightarrow 2 \rightarrow 3 \rightarrow 4 \rightarrow$ Present

Time

Progress is made stepwise.

FEYERABEND'S EPISTEMOLOGICAL ANARCHISM

Progress comes about through cross-pollination and chance.

Cause and Effect

Related to the principle of uniformity, but of much broader application, is the principle of causality. The nature of causes has been contentious throughout the history of philosophy, even resulting in serious disagreement between Plato and Aristotle. There are different formulations of this principle, some of them controversial, such as 'Every effect has a cause' or the more modest and Newtonian 'Every action results in some reaction'. Nevertheless, there has been general agreement that change of one kind or another requires a cause. In fact, it seems rather impossible to have a general theory of nature without appealing to causes and effects again and again. (See also section on Explanation vs Unification, in History of Principles above.)

Principles as Universals and Mathematical Formulas

We noted in the introduction that principles are often characterized in terms of mathematical notation. Part of the reason is for the precision which mathematical description affords, but it is also that mathematical formulas really capture universals well. A 'universal' means a statement that applies in all cases or at all times, or both. So 'Every X is a Y' is a kind of universal which can be mathematically formulated – for example, 'Every object that can be touched has atoms.' Even a statement like 'Gravity is constant' is saying something very much like 'All moments possess gravity', a universal declaration.

Despite the pull toward formalization, a misleading impression can be given by mathematical statements. 'A widow is a woman whose spouse has died' can very readily be understood as a universal statement and can be formalized mathematically as well. But a law of nature such as 'Ice is frozen water' is different from the statement about widows even though it seems the same on the surface. 'A widow is a woman whose spouse has died' is true by definition, whereas a principle of nature is true because it reflects a verifiable truth about the world. Unlike mathematical formulas, principles as laws of nature have a force which formalization by itself does not provide. This is because the necessity found in these laws is not the necessity of logic, but the necessity of the world as it happens to be.

Necessary and Contingent Truths

If the examples above make it difficult to appreciate the difference between logical truths and the laws of nature, the following explanation may clear things up a little. It is a known fact, due to the research of nuclear physicists, that a sphere of plutonium must be less than 1 kilometre (0.6 miles) in radius. The reason is that before plutonium can

PRINCIPLES OF NATURE AS CONTINGENT TRUTHS

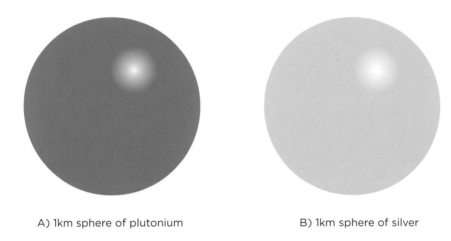

A) 1km sphere of plutonium   B) 1km sphere of silver

NEITHER A NOR B EXIST, BUT A IS PHYSICALLY IMPOSSIBLE SINCE
PLUTONIUM WOULD COLLAPSE BEFORE IT COULD REACH THAT SIZE.

approach anywhere near this mass it would immediately explode. Thus, it is a property of plutonium that if it exceeds a certain mass, it will necessarily resist getting any bigger. We can contrast this with the case of silver. As far as anyone knows, silver does not have any intrinsic properties which would prevent it from becoming 1 kilometre in radius or even longer. At the same time, it is a safe bet that nowhere in the universe is there a silver sphere 1 kilometre in radius, nor do we have the technology to be able to manufacture such a sphere.

So we can make statements about the silver and plutonium spheres which look on the surface identical:

1) All plutonium spheres are less than 1 km in radius.

2) All silver spheres are less than 1 km in radius.

However, as we have examined, the crucial difference is that the statement about plutonium is a law of nature whereas the statement about silver is not. The latter is a contingent fact about the silver that happens to be distributed in the universe. Nowhere in the universe, it turns out, is there such a huge accumulation of silver amounting to a

The search for understanding the principles of nature is an everlasting search.

1-kilometre sphere. With plutonium, on the other hand, it is simply not possible within the configuration of the present universe for a sphere of that metal to be 1 kilometre in radius. It is a feature of the universe and the plutonium in it that the mass of plutonium is limited in this way. The limit on plutonium is a law of nature while the limit on silver is merely happenstance.

Principles of Nature and You

We have seen that the search for the principles of nature has been undertaken and understood in very different ways. The earliest Greeks embarked on investigation to find out the truth of matter, while on Kuhn's reading of history, such a lofty aim was never possible – instead principles were posited as makeshift explanations as an attempt at consistency. And for someone like Hume, it is doubtful we can ever arrive at a justified reason to believe in principles of nature.

TRYING TO UNDERSTAND NATURE IS LIKE USING A TELESCOPE FROM WITH-IN THE UNIVERSE TO SEE THE UNIVERSE FROM THE OUTSIDE

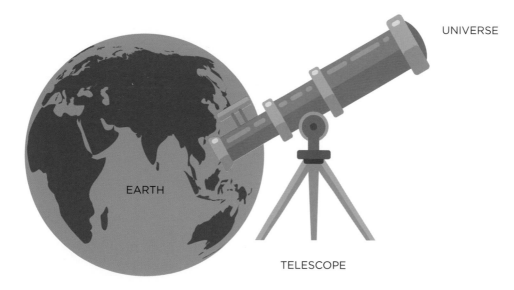

UNIVERSE

EARTH

TELESCOPE

Nature is all around us, and we are a part of nature; as I began this chapter, I noted how this makes understanding nature through its principles even harder. But it is also true that, of anything we wish to know, perhaps nothing is more important to us than to have knowledge of ourselves and of our world. It is inevitable that we seek principles to clarify and simplify this knowledge, and the never ending search for such principles is an indication that knowledge of principles is fundamental to human life.

SUMMARY POINTS

- The principles or laws of nature capture the regularity we see, or expect to see, in the world around us.
- The ancient Greeks were the first to seek principles of nature, some element valued as an explanation of the physical world.
- The principles which different Greek philosophers offered were usually physical elements like fire, water or air.
- The Stoic school of philosophy believed that the way the natural world was ordered was a guide to how we should live.
- In the 16th and 17th centuries scientists began to formulate laws of nature, based on testing and experimentation.
- John Locke criticized the possibility of knowledge about the principles of nature, on the grounds that we would have to know the kinds and effects of all atoms.
- The 'covering law' was a 20th-century attempt to explain how nature worked. All the cases under investigation were meant to fit in the explanation which a covering law provided.

Chapter 2

THE PRINCIPLES OF KNOWLEDGE

Knowledge of all kinds is so fundamental to how we live day to day that most people take it for granted. That is, it's as if knowledge or thinking is too important to think about because we are so busy thinking with it. This means the topic of the principles of knowledge can be very daunting, simply because we normally do not concern ourselves with how we think the way we do. Philosophy about knowledge is the field of 'epistemology', a Greek word meaning 'the study of knowledge'.

Questions on Knowledge

What is knowledge? How do we acquire knowledge, and how ought we acquire it? What is the relationship between our beliefs and knowledge? Do we have to justify our beliefs in order to have knowledge? Is knowledge even possible for human beings? These are some of the related questions central to the study of epistemology. Between the certainty of the dogmatic and doubts of the sceptic, there are many different positions to adopt when it comes to knowledge.

History of the Philosophy of Knowledge

The first formal study of knowledge can be found in Plato's Theaetetus, dating from around 400 BCE. In that dialogue knowledge is defined as that which is acquired through sensory perception. This thesis, 'Knowledge is perception' or something like it, has been advocated in different versions throughout the history of philosophy. It is not the only candidate, but it is a popular and very intuitive approach to identifying what knowledge is. After all, what is believing, if not seeing? We commonly employ the metaphor of 'seeing' or 'illumination' as a colourful way to say we are knowledgeable where we were not before. In Plato's dialogue the characters go through other candidates for knowledge and discuss how we justify the knowledge that we claim we have. The Theaetetus ends in a kind of philosophical draw – there are no definitive conclusions drawn about the right kind of epistemology, although certain liabilities are assigned to some theories.

KNOWLEDGE AS SIGHT

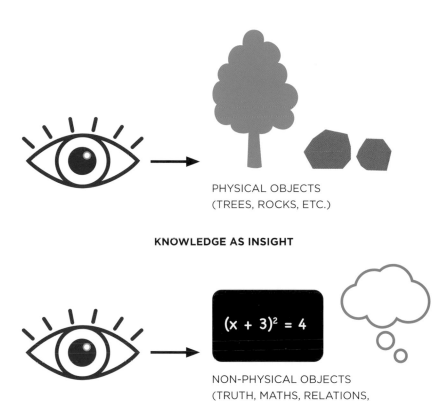

PHYSICAL OBJECTS
(TREES, ROCKS, ETC.)

KNOWLEDGE AS INSIGHT

$(x + 3)^2 = 4$

NON-PHYSICAL OBJECTS
(TRUTH, MATHS, RELATIONS,
THOUGHTS ETC.)

Truth, Lies, Appearances and Correspondence

Knowledge is closely related to truth. In ancient Greek the word for truth, *aletheia*, meant something like 'an un-hiding', or more literally a 'not escaping notice'. The concept of truth relates to what is really out there, as opposed to deception or illusion on the one hand, and as opposed to lies on the other.

TRUTH IS A 'REVEALING' AND DISCOVERY OF INFORMATION

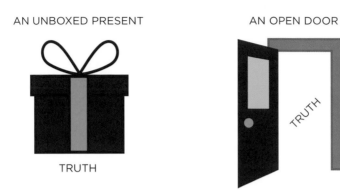

AN UNBOXED PRESENT   AN OPEN DOOR

TRUTH

TRUTH

In this Greek understanding of truth we see the kernel of what was later to be called the correspondence theory of truth. This theory posits that something (generally a statement) is true when it corresponds adequately to something in the real world, i.e. the facts. 'Delia's blue house is on Mulberry Street' is true if, in fact, Delia has a blue house standing there on Mulberry Street. Often when we want to emphasize the truth of something, we even talk in this way, saying 'it is a fact that…'.

THE CORRESPONDENCE THEORY OF TRUTH

'DELIA'S BLUE HOUSE IS ON MULBERRY STREET' IS TRUE, SINCE
HER HOUSE ACTUALLY IS ON MULBERRY STREET.

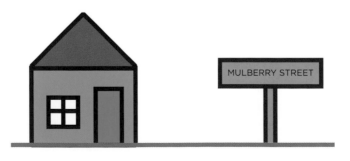

MULBERRY STREET

You have perhaps noted that in the above description of correspondence theory I qualified the correspondence by adding 'adequately'. This has led some to think that our relationship to truth is not one of direct access but that truth is represented by statements (or perhaps more broadly, language). Truth is mediated, or approximated, according to this way of understanding it.

One objection to the theory has been that it seems to treat facts, the things in reality by which a statement is judged true or false, as existing independently. This objection points out that it seems quite arbitrary to slice out a piece of reality, and then make statements about it. There can also be situations in which it is rather strange to claim that certain objects exist as real things if the statement is negative. Take, for example, the

'There are no leprechauns at the end of the rainbow' – is this a verifiable statement?

statement 'There are no leprechauns at the end of the rainbow'. Presumably this statement would be verifiable in the same way that 'Elephants are four-footed' is confirmed: one looks at the rainbow or the elephant to see if the reality matches up with the claim. What is odd is that the truth about the elephant can be readily confirmed – there is an elephant right here with four feet – but on the other hand, it is more than a little unusual to perceive as a physical fact that the leprechaun does not exist, as if this fact manifests as a reality in the same way that a palpable elephant does.

The Pragmatist View of Truth

Another way of conceiving of truth, or at least identifying truth, is the so-called Pragmatist view. This position is unique in that it sets aside the feature just discussed above, that truth depends on some objective state of affairs. Instead truth is recognized as the goal of a human-initiated inquiry. So when we have reached an answer adequate to whatever question we were asking or whatever problem we were seeking to solve, at that point we have achieved the truth.

Justification

As we continue on with the story of knowledge, it will probably be helpful to draw attention to 'justification' again. What does this term mean? Justification means the reason that we believe something to be true or that it is the case. For instance, we could believe

DOES THIS SCENE JUSTIFY A BELIEF IN A BANK ROBBERY?

BANK

that a bank is about to be robbed, but would it be justified? One person sees four men climb out of a car with masks and guns, look around and rush into the bank. Another person at another bank feels as if someone is going to rob him before he is able to deposit his cash. In the above scenarios, the first person would be justified in thinking there is a bank robbery occurring, while the second is simply suspicious, or possibly paranoid, because he is so preoccupied about his own money. We say the first person justified his belief because he has a reason and this reason directly correlates to the adoption of that belief in a way that the arbitrariness of paranoia does not.

Important Principles of Knowledge

Theories of knowledge can be laid out on the basis of several different – and often in-compatible – principles of knowledge. Keep in mind that proponents of these different theories are not always claiming that these are the only forms of knowledge, but that they are the best, or surest, kinds of knowledge we can have.

Perception as Knowledge

Seeing or hearing or feeling or tasting or smelling accounts for knowledge. If I look across the room and see a chair, then I am justified in having the belief 'There is a chair in the dining room' because I have had the visual perception of the chair. I need not appeal to anything other than my perception to ground my belief in the chair. I could likewise appeal to my sense of smell detecting the oak scent coming from the chair or my sense of touch feeling the corporeality of the chair and its peculiar wooden grain. It is important that within this framework the 'seeing of X' precedes 'believing in X'.

The knowledge that comes about through the senses has two parts. The first is more obvious. When we see a house, we have the house as an object of our vision. But there is a deeper way in which we are relying on the cognitive apparatus of our brains and eyes as visual organs. As soon as we introduce this into the equation, things immediately become more complicated. Perception is not something that just happens, simply and infallibly, on each occasion. It is a delicate relation between the perceiver and the perceived, in which the state of the perceiver must be in a certain condition (think of the impairment of a drunken person or one who is extremely sleepy) and the perceived object must be in a certain state as well (consider bad lighting, fog or a mirage).

There is thus a strong cognitive element in perception. Take the chair example from earlier. We see this object, and the object which causes the impression of 'chair' brings with it some conceptual baggage along for the ride; we do not merely see it as an object that happens to be the size and shape of a chair, as if sight were disconnected from our processing of what we see. The very fact that we are sometimes mistaken is a good indication of this – you think a coat-rack is a household intruder at the same moment as you spot the coat-rack in a dimly lit room. This is a good example of how perception has information embedded in itself – perceptions are rarely 'naked' and free of what we take them to be. In this particular case it was a mistake thinking an inanimate object was a threatening person. But it's not only at the moment of perception that objects of perception have a cognitive content; there can also be downstream beliefs dependent on the original perception. Let's say I see a coat-rack (this time correctly, as a coat-rack) and then later there is a fire by the only door leading outside. You try the window but it is stuck, so you take the coat-rack and use it as an impromptu battering ram to break the window. Your perception of the coat-rack has led to a new belief about it, perhaps even suggested to you because it resembles the shape and length of a real battering ram.

**PERCEPTION IS PRE-LOADED WITH CONCEPTS
– A COAT-RACK CAN BE SEEN AS AN INTRUDER**

COAT + HAT ON RACK   INTRUDER

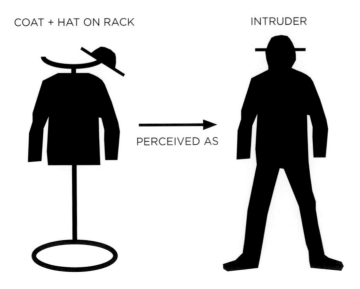

PERCEIVED AS

When we recognize that there are different elements in perceiving, it is easier to see that belief has a complex relationship to what is perceived. There is the blank unmediated data of the object itself, say green, ovoid-shaped and partly translucent. There is also a perception which exists at a level above, which tells me what the object is. In this case it is a leaf and I may even know what kind of leaf it is, say a cherry plum. At a level above this is the perception, 'Here is a leaf of a cherry plum.' One might think that this is not a perception, it is statement. But it is very difficult to look at objects, especially objects which are familiar to us through experience, and not perceive them 'as' something, a certain thing which has a place in our social and personal world. I may see a certain make and model of car, and immediately recognize it 'as' the car of my friend who is going to pick me up. When I do so, the perception of the car comes with certain associations, such as the goodness I feel when with the friend or the anticipation of going along on the ride. The activity of perception, as you can see, brings with it a lot of information – maybe the information is imposed on the perception, but at any rate the raw information of a perception, if such a thing even exists, is always processed through our minds such that it is given meaning, context, application, a judgement of value and innumerable other qualities as well. It does not appear that our eyes play one role and our minds another when we look out into or listen or touch the things in our world. Rather the eyes and mind work together, and any separation between them is indistinguishable in the common activity of sight. By analogy, we have good reason to think that the other sense perceptions work in the same way.

What are these objects? Our perception
tells us that they are cherry plum leaves.

Misidentification and Perception

If an act of perception does not straightforwardly *report* an object as it is, but rather perception *interprets* with near immediacy as soon as a perception occurs, then in what sense are perceptions reliable, and how can any perceptions be justified as knowledge? For instance, I might see a bird as a plane because it is so far away that I cannot distinguish its feathers or beak or even flight pattern. Am I justified in thinking this is a plane because it looks like a plane, even though it is really a bird? Misidentifications are a common liability of relying on sense perceptions, but optical illusions (seeing things that aren't actually there, such as a Bigfoot in the forest) or construing order when there

Perception risks deception: a horse-shaped cloud.

is none (seeing a cloud as a horse) are additional ways in which visual perception can deceive.

Nevertheless, in most general situations we are quite comfortable with relying on our senses to make it through life. Consider for a moment how many different times when driving a car we use our perception to avoid injury and even death. We must correctly perceive the colour of the traffic light to know when to go or stop, judge which objects are cars or pedestrians, and judge distances of varying lengths constantly. If navigating our world and avoiding death in the process is a kind of justification of perception as a source of knowledge, then our eyes are skilfully adequate even if imperfect.

Knowledge through Induction

Related to knowledge through perception is knowledge through induction. 'Induction' simply means that as we are exposed to more and more individual phenomena we tend to make generalizations or universal statements about them. These generalizations then are used as a framework to help us understand the world. For instance, if we see certain four-legged animals as we are growing up, we may come to call these creatures 'cats' and attribute distinct physical and personality traits to them, and in part this is done to distinguish them from dogs or horses.

Another way of describing what happens in induction is that we make an inference

INDUCTION LEADS US TO CONCLUSIONS

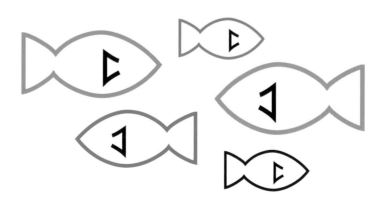

5 DIFFERENT FISH HAVE FINS: THEREFORE, 'FISH HAVE FINS'

about a thing or things which goes beyond the information immediately present. The information is magnified to apply to new cases or, more pervasively, all cases.

One type of induction, enumerative induction, aims at taking a limited amount of examples and extrapolating a conclusion. This is perhaps the most common form of evidence. In practical terms, it takes a representative sample and extrapolates the findings to apply to the whole. I conclude, based on the five different types of fish I have seen, that fish have fins.

Hypothetico-Deduction

In the scientific world, it is usual to employ this kind of induction to propose a tentative hypothesis, perhaps even based on the limited experience of a small sample size. Then 'deduction' (reasoning in the opposite direction, i.e. from generalizations to specific instances) is used to suggest results that might be expected if the hypothesis were true, and the hypothesis is subjected to further testing as to whether or not the proposed generalization holds true in every case.

Bayesian Epistemology

The foregoing examples of induction all deal with why we should or should not believe in a certain proposition. But there is another way to approach the topic of belief. This is to allow that there can be different degrees of belief. Belief can be strong or weak, or somewhere in between. Rooted in the thinking of 18th-century mathematician-philosopher Thomas Bayes, discussions about belief begin to take on a statistical aspect, since the probability of being true that we grant to a given belief correlates to the degree of certitude we have in that belief.

Memory as Knowledge

Let's say that I remember the day five years ago I stepped into a carpenter's shop and bought a chair. The chair I purchased is the one in the dining room over there, I think to myself. In this instance I have relied on memory and the use of my memory in forming a belief. I look into myself to form a belief – based on what I take to be knowledge about a past event, I apply it to a new instance and treat this as knowledge as well. But in contrast to looking out into the world through perception, I look into myself for the knowledge I seek, by focusing on my memory.

In our everyday life we often verify our memory, and in a very real sense give justification to our having a belief. For instance, I have a memory of making a sandwich to take to work with me. I have made so many sandwiches in the past that I begin to doubt whether I have made a sandwich on this day. Maybe I am mistaken. So I go to the refrigerator and I find a sandwich sitting in my lunch bag, just as usual. It seems I was justified in my belief I made a sandwich: it was there.

The degree to which we depend on memory for our beliefs is quite significant, since it involves to a large degree the totality of our past. We might think that we have many tools to help us with our memory, so we need not be entirely reliant on our conception of the past. Calendars, smart phones, internet cloud storage, photos – all of these serve to lessen the load on our memories, or so we think. But the truth is that even with these technologies, our faith in them depends on the degree to which we have memories of making them. If I do not remember having made an appointment for Thursday at 10.00 with the dentist, I have reason to not believe that I made the appointment at all, even if it has been input into my phone calendar. What this shows is that memory itself often serves as the justification for a belief. In the example above, memory served as justification for believing that I made a sandwich today. This is also confirmed by the fact that if I am aware I *lack* a memory of having made a sandwich today, I will be hesitant to hold the belief that I made one. We should pause for a second to note that this relationship between memory and belief is often taken for granted, without, at this point, weighing in on whether we should in fact rely on our memory to such a degree. For it could turn out that my wife made my sandwich today and placed it into the bag. When I see it, I erroneously come to the conclusion I have made it myself. Thus the memory of having made a sandwich on Tuesday becomes blurred into one of having made it today, Wednesday. As with many other forms of knowledge, it turns out that memory too is fallible. As memory can be wrong about the past, so perception can be wrong about the present.

Memory as Information

In the previous section we went over the way in which perception is information-laden. Whether at the source or developed through an inseparable process, perception brings with it information or interpretation of the data. In the same way, memory does not come without information. It is very difficult to hold a memory in our minds without affecting that memory in some way with alien material: we do not seem capable (or it is very rare and difficult) to think about something in our past just as it is, without embellishment, without subtraction, without judgements about good or bad. One paradox of memory seems to bring this out rather well. We have a memory of enduring a rather miserable experience some years ago. Perhaps it was very demanding labour, or a humiliating event. Often when looking back on such a day, it has a pleasantness that was never there in the event itself. We can even get a laugh out of the day, though there was nothing humorous about our experience. The retrieval and current experience of the memory are not quite the same as what the memory was about.

MEMORY RESHAPES OUR EXPERIENCE

PAST: FLAT TYRE IS BAD

PRESENT: FLAT TYRE IS PLEASANT, FUNNY TO REMEMBER

The way our memories facilitate our daily lives is not limited to episodes alone. Memories are constantly being searched, either explicitly or implicitly. Say you are in the car driving and start panicking that you have forgotten to pick up your prescription, which has just run out. What has happened is that you have become aware that there is no memory of having picked up the medicine. Memory is not treated as something external to yourself, to be tested or confirmed. It is a direct record of your personal experience, and this is why you act on your belief that it is true with immediate conviction. There is also the implication that memory covers all of our past, or at least claims to on some occasions. For when I realize I have forgotten to pick up my medicine today, I search the totality of my memory for any instance in the past on which I may have picked it up. The record of my memory sweeps through the halls of time and determines that no such occasion happened, and I behave on the basis of this belief, briefly panicking and determining to retrieve the medicine in the morning.

The Testimony of Others as Knowledge

It is a common experience to rely on the word of someone else, especially in relation to everyday life. You are in the kitchen and can't look at the moment, so you ask a visiting friend, 'Is there a chair in the dining room?' and she answers, 'Yes'. You take this to be a proper justification for thinking there is a chair because you trust your friend and you take this to be genuine knowledge. The kind of trust expected in these encounters is often not exceptional, and there are common examples of acquiring knowledge through testimony. We ask strangers all the time, 'What time is it?', 'Has the bus arrived yet?' and 'Is there somewhere I can find a good steak around here?'.

EVERY DAY WE RELY ON KNOWLEDGE ACQUIRED THROUGH TESTIMONY

When we do so, we expect an honest answer and take what we are told as solid knowledge. It is an open question whether this knowledge gained from the testimony of others is actually a distinct kind of knowledge, as ultimately it seems that testimony arises from something other than testimony itself. For example, if I trust my friend who told me that there is a chair in the dining room, she presumably came to this conclusion because she saw the chair herself. Despite this acknowledgement, we still might consider testimonial knowledge to be an independent source of knowledge because when we use this kind of knowledge we do not have access to the source from which our testifier has gained their knowledge.

What counts as testimonial knowledge, besides the fact that it has to arise from a testifier? The first is that it has to arise directly from testimony. That is, it has to be communicated directly from one person to another in some form, usually orally or written. An interesting distinction in this regard is that there has to be a certain amount of trust invested in the testifier for this knowledge to be testimonial. Consider a scenario in which John tells Maria he can do an amazing Tom Cruise impression. Maria thinks that this is very unlikely given John's husky, gravelly voice. But John says to her, shockingly, 'Show me the money' in Tom Cruise's voice. In this instance John has *shown* Maria directly that he could pull off the impression, in the same way that he could have shown her his ability to juggle five balls at once, after insisting to her that he could do so. But only if Maria believed that John could do the impression or juggle the balls, not because he *showed* he could do so, but because he *told* her he was going to do so, would this count as testimonial knowledge.

The most common scenario for testimony is that between a testifier or speaker and a hearer, so I will make use of this speaker/hearer dynamic although other forms of communication are possible as well. In order for the testimony to count as knowledge, the speaker must actually possess the knowledge that will be conveyed to the hearer. It cannot be untrue, misleading or otherwise disqualified as knowledge. The second step in this scenario is that the hearer must come to believe the testimony because of the content of what the speaker has said. The content of the testimony is like a baton being passed between two runners in a relay race. Knowledge is transmitted from one person to another, wholly preserved as it makes this journey. Nothing substantial is either added or taken away.

Sometimes a further qualification is added: that the hearer must have no unanswered objections against believing the content of what the speaker has presented. Such objections may be psychological. Imagine that you are watching an air show with different types of aircraft flying by. You see a jet pass and think to yourself, 'That's an F-15.' Later on you see the same jet dart through the sky again and your friend says, 'Those F-35s are incredible machines!' This remark undermines your confidence that the plane you saw was an F-15. It doesn't matter whether you or your friend is right in this instance. The only thing that matters is that your friend's remark has undermined the intellectual consistency of your account. Even if you turn out to be right, and you did see an F-15 and not an F-35, your belief is hardly justified given what your friend has said – assuming you have no special

Is this an F-15 or an F-35? Would your belief be undermined by another's statement?

background knowledge of aircraft. In addition to psychological objections, there are normative objections. We can change the scenario above so that your friend is a retired officer from the air force. He says, 'Wow, look at that F-35,' but you ignore his expertise and stubbornly cling to the conviction that it is an F-15. Nonetheless your belief that the plane is an F-15 is undermined by the evidence your friend has offered.

Justification of Testimony

A variation of the testimonial view of knowledge is that the information being conveyed is what is relevant, so it can even be transmitted without any conviction from a first person lacking belief to a second who does have a committed belief. This leads us to the topic of the justification of testimonial knowledge, or the way in which testimony is a valid way to acquire knowledge.

There are two streams of thought on how testimony is justified. The first is to say that testimony need not be justified in terms of another kind of knowledge, such as perception or memory. Testimony is considered to be on a par with other modes of knowing, and relevantly distinct, so it does not have to be vetted to confirm it is passing on knowledge of some more elementary form. The other feature from earlier in the discussion still stands:

KNOWLEDGE FROM TESTIMONY

I CAN JUGGLE

JOHN SPEAKING

MARIA IS LISTENING

DIRECT KNOWLEDGE: NOT KNOWLEDGE FROM TESTIMONY

JOHN JUGGLING

MARIA WATCHING

the belief in testimony must not have any unanswered objections still outstanding.

On the other side there is the position that testimony is reliable, or should be believed in, only when it can be justified in terms of other kinds of knowledge. The scope of this is quite broad, but simply put, it means that testimony can be believed when it can be corroborated by other sources.

A *Priori* Knowledge

Suppose I see the chair, and I look at its four legs. In my imagination I construct a square drawn between the four feet of the chair and conclude that the angles making up the corners of this square add up to 360 degrees. Now, this belief of mine owes to *a priori* knowledge. This is a Latin phrase meaning 'beforehand' which tells us that the knowledge is independent of experience. That is, the knowledge that the angles of the square created between the legs of the chair add up to 360 degrees comes about not because we have measured that this is so, but because of the very definition of a square. There is no appeal to our memory or to what the five senses have delivered to us. This knowledge comes about through reason itself, without any need for experience, merely by relying on the relationships between concepts. Often knowledge that comes from this reliance on reason alone has been contrasted with what has been taken to be its opposite, knowledge through the senses.

One way to explain the concept of the *a priori* is that there can be no further demonstration, evidence or generally any kind of reason why it is the case that these angles of a square add up to 360 degrees. It is simply self-evident that this is the case; it is a brute fact about the universe and logic that this geometrical truth is the way it is.

One of the drawbacks of this form of knowledge is that it apparently does not apply to a lot of objects or issues we commonly encounter day to day. For this reason, some have thought that *a priori* knowledge, depending on rationality alone, uniquely offers knowledge in its surest form, or on the other hand, that any system of knowledge should begin with the truths accessible through *a priori* means.

If you construct a square between the four legs of the chair in your imagination, you have a priori knowledge that the angles of the square add up to 360° – you don't need to measure them.

An important clarification about the notion of the *a priori* is that it is a claim about the type of knowledge, not about its acquisition. Experience does contribute when it comes to certain information needed to acquire *a priori* knowledge. Subsequent to this acquisition of the concepts used in a priori reasoning, however, there is no reliance on experience, only on the relations and inferences which can be made among the concepts themselves.

All of the different forms of knowledge discussed above can be kinds of epistemology. Indeed, these ways of knowing are the most commonly appealed-to modes of knowledge. However, it should be kept in mind that, although there are philosophers who advocated one mode of knowing as the best, most important or fundamental, the reality is that most of these forms of knowledge are used by us everyday as the circumstances arise. Equally important is that when it comes to epistemology there is an unspoken assumption that the knowledge is centred on the individual, who is considered the locus of responsibility and the centre of knowledge.

Empiricism vs Rationalism

A big division in the history of epistemology has been the empiricist/rationalist divide. This is not a dispute about whether we gain knowledge through experience or through reason, but about whether knowledge is justified or grounded through experience or through reason. For example, empiricists claim that even rationalist truths are ultimately dependent on empirical knowledge, just as some rationalists ground all truths in truths of reason alone. Between these views there are more or less moderate views, sometimes attributing more importance to their own view but not denying that the other side provides grounds for at least some knowledge.

Epistemology assumes that knowledge is focused on the individual.

Knowledge, Ignorance and Scepticism

Along with knowledge comes the default state of human life, ignorance. Studying the nature of ignorance will tell us a lot about what we think knowledge is, but even if we understand minimally that ignorance is a lack of knowledge, we understand both that ignorance comes before knowledge and that knowledge has to be acquired in some way. Knowledge doesn't come about without some activity or, in many cases, hard work. Consider as examples a challenging maths exam or trying to find out someone's personality through dating.

The difficulty of acquiring knowledge and the persistence of ignorance have caused some to think that the pursuit of knowledge is a dead end. Scepticism, the belief that humans cannot acquire knowledge, has had quite a long history, going back as far as the beginnings of Western philosophy in ancient Greece. Some schools of philosophy have taken the very fact that different philosophers historically offered different and incompatible accounts of how to acquire knowledge as proof that the nature of knowledge cannot be reliably uncovered. If even the great minds of philosophy cannot agree about the truth of knowledge, then what hope does the average John or Jane have of finding out the truth of the matter?

IGNORANCE	KNOWLEDGE
ABSENCE OF INFORMATION	PRESENCE OF INFORMATION
PRIOR TO KNOWLEDGE	AFTER IGNORANCE
SIMPLE	COMPLEX

Principles of Knowledge and You

Knowledge is contrasted with both ignorance and what is false. Since much of our personal and business life concerns avoiding ignorance and falsehood, then it seems reasonable that we should have a strong interest in what knowledge is all about. This means we need to know what forms knowledge comes in – memory, perception, *a priori* and so forth – so that we can accurately test the information we have gained in accordance with the way we acquired the knowledge. Assessing the strength of the information we have is vital in using that information the right way.

A second aspect of knowledge is the credence we grant to different information. The strength we accord to any belief or information not only depends on the source or the credibility of the person conveying it, but also importantly depends on the use to which we will put the information. Asking someone whether there is a supermarket at the next junction is quite a different question from asking someone whether or not they have properly packed the parachute you are about to use. The trust and credibility of the parachute-packer is of a higher degree than someone pointing to the nearest supermarket, because the first determines only whether you can buy groceries soon and the second whether you will live.

We need a much higher degree of trust in the parachute-packer than in the person directing us to the nearest supermarket.

SUMMARY POINTS

- The acquisition, possession and justification of knowledge is known as the field of epistemology.
- Truth is the lynchpin of knowledge; it is what we aim at and we judge if something is truthful on whether it captures truth or not.
- The correspondence theory of truth states that something is true if it matches up to the facts of reality.
- The pragmatist view of truth defines truth as that which adequately answers a question posed by human enquiry.
- Justification is the warrant for possessing knowledge.
- Knowledge through induction reaches a generalization through observations.
- Bayesian epistemology posits that there can be different degrees of conviction in someone's beliefs.
- Testimonial knowledge is formed from reports of others.
- *A priori* knowledge comes about directly from the mind, by understanding the relationships of concepts and ideas, such as geometrical truths.
- Empiricism is the position that experience justifies our knowledge, while rationalism is the position that reason justifies our knowledge.
- Ignorance shows us that knowledge follows after ignorance and that knowledge has to be acquired in some way.

Chapter 3

THE PRINCIPLES OF METAPHYSICS

In previous chapters we discussed the nature of reality, primarily as understood in the immediate sense of what is before us in this physical universe. The investigation into the nature of reality has led many philosophers to posit unseen realities as underlying the visible. In a broad sense, that is what the field of metaphysics is concerned with.

The word 'metaphysics' itself captures in a nutshell the meaning of the discipline. Among many other books, Aristotle wrote a *Physics* as well as a *Metaphysics*. The story goes that the book which we now call *Metaphysics* was placed after the book called *Physics* on a bookshelf. This is what the word *metaphysics* in Greek means: 'after physics'. However, it is more likely that the naming of this book was not just a happenstance coinage from the layout of Aristotle's library, since the Greek prefix *meta* can also mean 'beyond'. 'Beyond physics' is an apt description of the field of metaphysics, for it seeks to go beyond the particular to universals, beyond the visible to the invisible, beyond the shallow appearance of things into the deep underlying reality.

ARISTOTLE'S LIBRARY

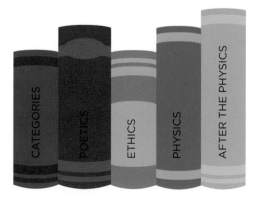

CATEGORIES POETICS ETHICS PHYSICS AFTER THE PHYSICS

Aristotle, as the formal originator of the field of metaphysics, said it was the study of 'being *qua* being'. What he meant by this is that metaphysics is an investigation into reality of whatever it is which happens to exist. In the broadest sense, metaphysics studies the nature of what is out there, and for this very reason it often deals in universals, that is, general concepts or principles which apply or are meant to describe the reality of the universe. In fact, Aristotle is famous for having enumerated ten very broad 'categories' as a way to capture and classify everything that exists.

Aristotle also characterizes metaphysics in another way, loading the field with a gravity and scope which many have embraced and others have shunned. On this conception, metaphysics is 'first philosophy' as measured by importance, and is synonymous with theology, the study of the divine.

Questions

What is there? Is the universe one thing or many things? If the universe is made of many things, how many things are there, and how do we categorize them? Is everything that exists made out of physical matter? Do things really exist as they appear, or is it an illusion? What is ultimate reality? What are the ultimate building blocks of this reality, if any?

History of Philosophy of Metaphysics

The study of metaphysics, like all philosophy, is bound up with human language (as was evident in Aristotle's categorization). This means that the discussion of metaphysics is necessarily bound up with certain expressions, ways of articulating these complex and abstract concepts. But it does not mean that metaphysics is reducible to mere words or is to be straightforwardly identified with wordplay. Rather it is an identification of the way in which metaphysical discussions are very complex and the way the language we use must be carefully crafted to match the subject matter.

Plato's Particulars and Forms

Discussion about metaphysical truths took place well before Plato, but he is significant for bringing into focus the relationship between what we today call particulars and universals. Like all of us, Plato looked out into his world and saw instances of what we would agree are the same kind: horses, trees, people, ships, tables, chairs, houses. Let's take horses from this list as an example. You see different horses trotting in a field. Some

Plato.

are black, others are white, some are dappled. No two are exactly alike in size or shape either. Yet we call each one of them a 'horse' with the same legitimacy. This is where we must be careful to acknowledge that we are not talking about mere names or words. The position Plato took is that all these animals are individual instances of the thing we call a horse, and there is one entity over and above all these instances, which accounts for why they are horses and why we give them this name. The individuals we call 'particulars' while the single entity over them all is the 'universal'. Plato gave the universal a privileged place, claiming that the universal was the very reason for the existence of particulars, and that particulars were inferior copies of the original universal. This relation of universals to particulars has come to be known as Plato's theory of Forms.

The theory of Forms has a been an influential and controversial idea in the history of metaphysics, but it also reveals the pull that many people have to try to reconcile particular instances with a universal idea. This is reflected not only in our language, since we think that a poodle is a 'dog' no less than a chihuahua is a 'dog', but also in our understanding of the world: we assign a label and a conceptual place to something when we have allocated it to the correct universal category.

PLATO'S THEORY OF FORMS

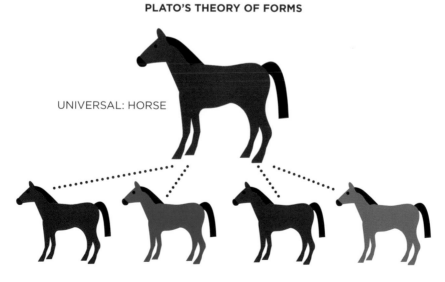

UNIVERSAL: HORSE

PARTICULARS: HORSE

The sun is a star – with star being the universal.

Aristotle on Universals

Both Plato and Aristotle were aware of the role language played in expressing metaphysical ideas. Aristotle formulated his discussion of the relationship between particulars and universals as simple statements of the form 'A is X'. Take, for example, 'The sun is a star', where the particular is the sun and star is the universal. On both Plato and Aristotle's understanding, the sun 'partakes' of the universal, star, in the sense that when we say that sun 'is' a star, we are assigning the sun to the category of star.

Monism

Another very important idea in the development of metaphysics, not just in antiquity but continuing up to the present, is the concept of monism. This is the belief that what exists is just one thing, or that just one kind of thing accounts for the makeup of the whole universe. In Chapter 1 we saw that pre-Socratic philosophers often posited some single physical element as the source of the universe, such as air or water. These physical principles were a sort of proto-monism, a suggestive movement toward the idea that the universe consists of only one single thing.

There were different advocates of monism of one stripe or another in ancient Greece, but the most famous was Parmenides. Parmenides composed an elaborate mythological poem in defence of his monism. Of particular importance, he argued that the universe was a single, unchangeable thing and furthermore that there was no such thing as non-existence. This seems a rather odd thing to think, but it was in line with Parmenides' radical adherence to consistency. If there really is one thing that exists, then there can be no room for anything else to exist, even if that thing is non-existence. Parmenides pointed out that non-existence does not exist as something, because it *is not*. There is controversy in the analysis of his complex claims, but the intended scope of his monism was so totalizing that it reignited the debate between pluralism and monism in ancient Greece.

Parmenides.

Atomism

Perhaps the greatest assault on monism in antiquity came from the atomists, Leucippus and Democritus. Parmenides had discounted the possibility of anything existing other than the singularity of the universe as an unchanging whole. This even excluded the possibility of motion or change, which required a transition from one thing into

Leucippus.

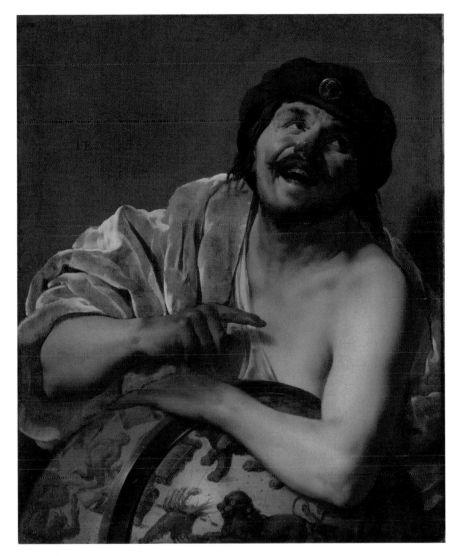

Democritus.

another. The atomists said that non-being does exist, in the form of the void. Reality is divided into two parts, atoms and the void. The atoms are being and the void is the non-being in which the atoms are given space to move and otherwise change. With Plato and Aristotle coming on the scene, the study of metaphysics would shift focus to discussions not only about the nature of the universe but the nature of individual everyday objects as well.

THE ATOMIST UNIVERSE

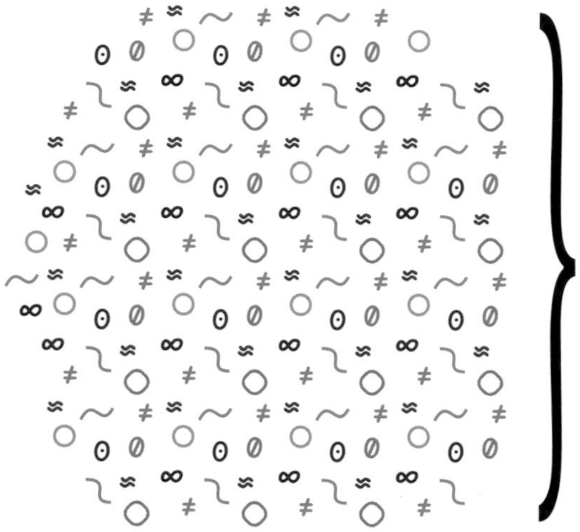

ATOMS
FALLING
DOWN
THROUGH
THE
VOID

Aristotelian Substance

Let's return to perhaps the central idea in Aristotle's concept of categories, that of substance. His concept of a substance is admirable not only because it seems to reflect our common understanding of what things are, but also for the consistency of application his theory provides.

When we walk into a new supermarket for the first time, we want to know the layout of the shop, where dairy and beverages and bread and meat have been displayed. We take for granted that the items we want to buy are 'real' things. Perhaps we even think that some things are more real and so have more of a claim on the term 'substance' than do others. A piece of lint seems to be less of a substance than is a person, for example. If this makes sense to you, this is part of the intuitive appeal informing Aristotle's theory of substances.

Aristotle says that an individual person is a substance, and this would further be qualified as an example of a 'primary substance'. What does Aristotle have in mind with this language? First let's discuss how he differentiates a primary substance, such as a person or a horse. He says the thing in question has to be a single thing and able to serve as the subject of different qualities. By different qualities he means that Socrates or Deborah are primary substances because they are individuals and they can be hot or cold, tan or pale, knowledgeable or ignorant. In other words, their position as a single subject allows them to change from one quality to its opposite while still remaining the same bearer of those qualities.

For Aristotle, the primary substance is the individual, whether it be a tree, horse or human. Socrates is a primary substance. But what about the category of human? This too merits the name of substance, but secondary substance, because the reality of the secondary substance depends on that of the primary substance for its existence.

ARISTOTELIAN SUBSTANCE PRIORITIZES THE INDIVIDUAL HORSE

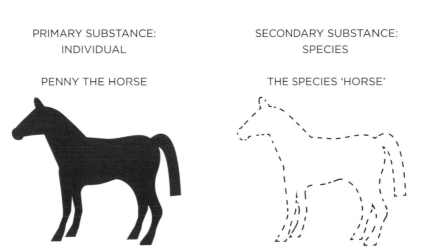

PRIMARY SUBSTANCE:
INDIVIDUAL

SECONDARY SUBSTANCE:
SPECIES

PENNY THE HORSE

THE SPECIES 'HORSE'

Form and Matter

Another very influential metaphysical concept introduced by Aristotle was his doctrine of hylomorphism. The word simply means 'matter' plus 'form'. With these two aspects Aristotle was able to capture in a broad way what makes a thing what it is. The form is that which gives the thing its shape, character or definition, while its matter is its physical makeup or what constitutes it. So a statue is made of bronze, and its shape is that of Hercules, or the matter of a house is bricks while its shape is the architectural structure. What's important from Aristotle's point of view is that these are not just two elements slapped together. The form, as the essence of the thing, determines how the matter will be arranged. So the form of Hercules determines the arrangement and kind of matter the artist has to use to create a statue. Aristotle intends his hylomorphic analysis to apply to living things as well. Of particular interest is that he says the soul is the form of the body, which is the matter.

Matter and Form:

Aristotle's hylomorphism – you can capture the nature of a thing by describing its matter and form – in this case the statue's matter is bronze and its form is Hercules.

Universals in Medieval Times: Genera and Species

So far, in going through some key metaphysical ideas in Plato and Aristotle, we have seen that they both engaged with 'universals' but in different ways. Universals, remember, are ways of grouping singular instances into more general concepts. Plato made his universals into Forms. There is a Form of Chair, for example, which a particular chair can never measure up to, since the Form of the Chair is perfect, timeless and never changes. On the other hand Aristotle turned this formulation on its head, making the individual chair the true reality, as opposed to the universal. The universal, the category of chair, is consigned by Aristotle to have less priority – it is a secondary substance – while the individual chair is the primary substance.

Between these two views there still remain many important questions. Are universals and particulars real things, or are they just conceptual shortcuts which allow us to understand things that would ordinarily overwhelm us? Taking a cue from the Platonic–Aristotelian divide, are particulars or universals more primary? What is the relationship between genera and species?

GENUS AND SPECIES

GENUS: CHAIR: FURNITURE FOR SITTING

FOLDING CHAIR RECLINER THRONE

THREE SPECIES OF CHAIR AS DEFINED BY DIFFERENT USES

The conversation about these and related questions exploded during the medieval period. The questions about genera and species can be viewed as an elaboration on the investigation between universals and particulars. A species (not the scientific, biological sense as applied to plants and animals) was understood in comparison to another species of the same genus. So, to use a modern example, a folding chair (species) shares the genus 'chair' with a recliner chair (another species). Both are chairs, and both fall under the genus 'chair', which captures their similarity to each other, while they nevertheless retain certain differences. The recliner can recline, has fabric, is heavy, and so forth. All of these qualities, and those of the folding chair, are *differentiae*, a Latin word which simply means 'differences', and these are what distinguish them.

Abelard and the Beginning of Nominalism

In the debates about the relationship between universals and particulars, some philosophers attempted to preserve the Platonic idea that universals exist independently of the particulars which exemplify them. The proponents of these views were deemed 'realists' since they attributed real existence to universals. Peter Abelard (1079–1142) weighed in on this dispute by attacking the independence of universals. His overall strategy was to deny that universals had a robust, substantial existence; instead he said that they are mental items which exist only in words.

Peter Abelard.

According to Abelard's view, the confusion we get from universals arises in part from the ambiguous way in which the same noun can apply to a particular and a universal. For instance, the word 'man' refers to the man sitting over there on the park bench eating a tuna sandwich. But 'man' also signifies the category to which every individual man belongs. There is a conceptual confusion because we use the same word with two different applications. In Abelard's words, the particular man is designated by 'man' as a 'mode of existence'. That is, this man on the bench actually exists as a real person. By contrast, the 'man' as in 'man is a noble animal' is a 'mode of signification'. It does not refer to a singular existing person, but signifies a kind of universality. One problem Abelard faced was how to answer the objection that his view required a subjective view of universals. That is, if 'man' in the sense of a universal category is simply a signification, how do we know what it does or should signify? It's simply a mental construct, so we very well might have different things in mind when I say 'man' and you say 'man'. To solve this, Abelard posited that these universals existed as ideas in the mind of God, and with this move he was able to confer an objective meaning upon them.

Abelard and his later followers came to be called by the term 'nominalists' after the Latin word for 'word' or 'name', since they denied universals existed in the robust Platonic sense. Instead they affirmed merely the 'words' or 'names' conferred on universals.

Duns Scotus

For quite a while after the death of Abelard, the realists held the day, and the spectre of nominalism faded. However, new discussions were providing important distinctions and variations on the old ideas. John Duns Scotus (1266–1308) contributed to this dialogue on universals and particulars. Following a line of thinking first developed by Thomas Aquinas, Scotus focused on the idea of nature. There are natures to individuals, and we can refer to these natures as real entities existing over and above individuals. He called these 'common natures'.

John Duns Scotus.

He had several arguments against the nominalist position but perhaps the most compelling appeals to our experience with everyday objects. We see a single bee and a butterfly among the flowers of the garden. Numerically there is one of each, and they can be compared on this basis. Another bee comes among the flowers and now we have two bees and a butterfly. We can perform a similar comparison between the two bees, as again there is one of each. In Scotus' terminology they have 'numerical unity'. But he also believed there is something beyond this numerical unity when we compare the bees to each other as contrasted with the butterfly: we think the bees have something in common with each other which the butterfly does not share. Scotus said that this element in common was also a kind of unity. The bees have numerical unity, since they are both singular, but they also have a unity of being the same species.

DUNS SCOTUS' UNIVERSALISM

TWO BEES: 'NUMERICALLY SAME'

COMPARED TO A BUTTERFLY THE BEES ARE 'SPECIFICALLY SAME'

William of Ockham

William of Ockham (1287–1347) represented the nominalist side, going so far as to say that everything in the world is singular and there are no universals: universals were nothing more than the imaginary language tools of the mind. Echoing similar language in Abelard, he explained universals as signifiers of meaning while denying they had any substantial existence. Even universals, by his explanation, were individual things.

Ockham believed that when we form a universal in our mind, what happens is that we acquire the idea of a flower from seeing one flower. This singular concept of a flower then 'stands in for', or 'supposits for' in William's terminology, all the subsequent instances of flowers which we encounter. What appears to a be universal when we say 'Flowers are pretty' or 'Roses are flowers' is simply a manner of talking about certain individual flowers.

Entities should not be needlessly multiplied

Pater Ockim

WILLIAM of OCCAM c.1285-1349
Doctor Invincibilis

William of Ockham.

René Descartes.

René Descartes

Descartes (1596–1650) marks a watershed in the history of philosophy, especially with regard to epistemology and metaphysics. His philosophizing is positioned right at the border of medieval philosophy – on the brink of the Enlightenment – and was heavily influenced by the scholastic debates and assumptions preceding him. He is famous, perhaps infamous, in philosophy for his advocacy of strict separation between the body and soul. The conclusions Descartes drew, that the soul is entirely different from the body and that humans are to be identified with our soul more than our body, continue to be influential today.

According to Descartes, our human essence is to be identified with our soul because we can introspect and discover this truth by the experience of thinking. The distinction that Descartes laid out was between the soul, which was a 'thinking thing', and matter, which was an 'extended thing'. His argument depends on the fact that we have a clear and distinct appreciation that we are thinking things, and that this quality of our thinking depends in no way on the existence of a body or our existing within a body.

For our purposes, one of the general points of interest in Descartes as a metaphysician is the intimate way in which introspection leads to his metaphysical conclusions. For instance, he asks us to suppose we do not exist. You attempt to do so, yet how is it possible

CARTESIAN DUALISM

BODY – EXTENDED MATTER   MIND – THINKING THING

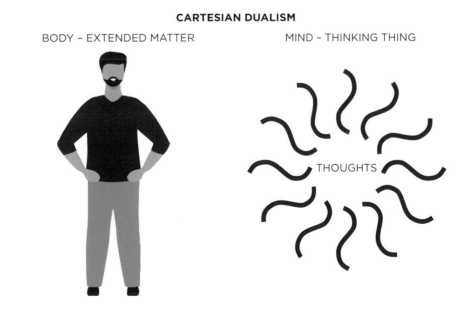

THOUGHTS

for you not to exist when you are right here *supposing* 'I do not exist', when the activity of supposing requires that there is an existing person who is doing that supposing? This is his argument for confirming we exist, and his case for concluding that we are thinking things is similar. Let's suppose we are not thinking things as humans. But in trying to suppose we are *not* thinking things we are in fact *thinking* about this idea. In trying to show we are not thinking things, we demonstrate to ourselves that we really are thinking things. As with the debate between nominalists and realists, there was a reaction to Descartes' advocacy of metaphysical dualism, the position that soul and body are two different substances. One of the rivals to this proposal was that soul and body, along with everything else, consisted purely of matter.

Thomas Hobbes

More famous for his *Leviathan*, a work of enormous influence in political philosophy, Thomas Hobbes (1588–1679) also had metaphysical convictions, responding in part to Descartes' metaphysics. In contrast to Descartes, Hobbes denied that anything besides matter existed. This is especially noteworthy because of the theological implication that spiritual beings, even God himself, are made of matter.

One reason Hobbes argued that everything is matter is that when we think, all of the content of our thought consists of images. These images, he insists, only arise from physical things we have seen with our own eyes. We can form no image of something we have not seen and, simply put, in order to be seen, something has to exist as matter in the world. He offers up the example of angels, which we conjure up as an image of a flame or perhaps a 'pretty little boy with wings'. Hobbes also extended this idea to God, and came under the charge of a kind of atheism by asserting that God has body. The exact way in which God is a body is hard to discern. For Hobbes seems to think both that God is diffused throughout the universe and that he has a 'simple corporeal spirit'.

By Hobbes' reckoning, time and space do not exist in the strict sense, because they exist only in the mind. His argument for showing this was quite ingenious: he claimed that if space itself were an object, then there would be no room for other objects to be in space, since two objects cannot exist in the same spot without one displacing the other.

From the perspective of philosophy, Hobbes shows how the adoption of a single idea – all is matter – has a metaphysical impact on the way even theology and physics are interpreted.

Baruch Spinoza.

Gottfried Leibniz.

Baruch Spinoza

If Hobbes' metaphysical philosophy was an attempt to explain the material basis of all reality as one physical stuff, Baruch Spinoza (1632–1677) can be said to have turned this hypothesis on its head, by supposing that there is only a single substance, God, and everything in the universe is a different mode of God.

We should begin by defining substance and mode. They are mutually exclusive categories: something cannot be both a substance and a mode. Furthermore, anything which cannot be considered to be either a substance or a mode is only a 'rational being', meaning that it exists only in the human mind, as a concept. Spinoza's definition of substance is similar to Aristotle's view: a substance is that which does not belong to anything else (in the sense of being describable as a feature of it). Furthermore a substance has an essential autonomy – the definition of a substance does not depend on any other thing.

A mode is something which can be understood as the quality, affection or state of a substance. As contrasted with the independence of a substance, a mode is completely dependent upon a substance both in terms of being conceived and its existence.

Echoing the two-fold distinction of Descartes, Spinoza also said there was thought and spatial extension. He called these the 'attributes' of a substance, the only attributes knowable by humans. These two attributes are essentially different, and in a parallel way to that in which substances are not dependent on modes for their definition, so also thought and spatial extension are not dependent on each other for their definition.

In Spinoza's system the ultimate reason for all things is God's essence. God's essence possesses an infinite quantity of attributes (all but two of which are inaccessible to us).

Gottfried Leibniz

In Leibniz (1646–1716) we see another pre-eminent philosopher grappling with the issue of the soul (sometimes termed the 'mind') and body. In particular, beginning with Descartes' strict separation between soul and body, a new problem popped up. It seems from common experience that our soul influences our body and our body influences our soul. We can state this more formally as the body and soul 'cause' each other to do certain things. For example, the mind causes the leg to move or, from body to mind, the skin causes the mind to feel the sensation of itching. But if the mind and body are entirely two different things, how is it that the one can cause the other to do something? Leibniz's surprising move was to reject the very idea that mind and body can influence each other, declaring that only God can do such a thing.

Important Principles of Metaphysics

Principle of Sufficient Reason

One of the most famous principles in metaphysics and epistemology is the principle of sufficient reason (PSR): that everything has a cause or reason behind it. Historically this was widely held as a philosophical starting point. It is a presumption that directly touches on a metaphysical faith in the nature of reality and arguably implies that we are able to acquire this information about anything.

At the beginning of ancient Greek philosophy it was taken for granted that the universe, all of existence, had to come from something. There had to be an explanation for the way things are. Similarly, the fact that as children we are constantly asking 'why?' is a good indication of the intuitive appeal of the principle of sufficient reason.

Leibniz gives a clear articulation of the principle: 'We consider that we can find no true or existent fact, no true assertion, without there being a sufficient reason why it is thus and not otherwise, although most of the time these reasons cannot be known to us.' A few different variations of this principle can be formulated. One is that the principle of sufficient reason is meant to offer an explanation of a specific causal event such that it is necessary things turn out a given way.

The scope of the PSR is probably the single best feature to bring out its nature. It is meant to apply to everything in the universe which ever has or will exist. So it is not even possible to find some object or scenario which does not have an explanation of some kind – this is what is required by the principle itself.

A- and B-Theories of Time

In the first century CE St Augustine said that time is something we all know, but as soon as we come to thinking about it, this assurance as to its nature quickly escapes us. Despite our deep experiential interaction with time, it remains a very difficult subject to think about. By the early 20th century, John M.E. McTaggart was proposing that there are two different models of time, and his distinction offers insights into time itself even though he rejected both models.

The A-theory of time fairly represents the average person's conception of it. Time is 'tensed' on this view, meaning that there really is an objectively existing time called the *present* which is what everything is experiencing simultaneously right at this instant. Thus to call time tensed is to say that the future really is yet to come and the past is really what has happened, considered from this perspective we call the present. The B-theory of time, on the other hand, rejects the idea that time is tensed. The A-theory, from the perspective of the B-theorist, is simply describing a psychological feature of how humans perceive time. B-theory proposes that time is not one privileged moment which is always changing, which we name the present or the 'now', but that all the past, present and future are part of one unified whole, and are equally real. Time, along with space, are a part of a continuous block. The past, present and future are not to be understood as times in relation to a privileged present but as relative to each other in a before, later and simultaneous relationship.

Soul-and-Body Interaction

Earlier we discussed how Descartes grappled with the possibility of mind-and-body interaction, a relationship which appears to have been made more difficult to describe as a result of his radical separation between the immaterial mind and material body. Soul–body interaction has received a fair amount of attention since Descartes' time, especially because it tends to involve theological questions about the existence of an immortal soul. At the heart of this so-called soul/body dualism is the worry that these two substances have almost nothing in common, and so there is a problem with how one can influence the other. How does what is immaterial 'move' what is material, given that it has no physical means by which to push, pull or otherwise manipulate it?

Occasionalism

To say this is a difficult question without easily obtained answers is an understatement, but it would be helpful to sketch out the two most popular approaches to this metaphysical question. One approach is to say that in some way body and soul can influence each other causally. Nicolas Malebranche in the 17th century offered up a novel explanation for the way that soul and body interacted. According to his theory, the body and mind are incapable on their own of reaching out to causally influence the other substance, with which they have nothing in common. Instead, when I have the thought to move my arm, God steps in, as it were, to move my arm; and in the other direction, if I step on a sharp rock, the pain delivered to my foot is not caused properly by the rock, but by God. These two scenarios are considered 'occasions' on which God steps in to produce the effects we see, such as the movement of the arm or pain in the foot. This was deemed the philosophy of 'occasionalism' as a result.

Transcendental Idealism

We have seen how the study of metaphysics is an inquiry into ultimate reality. Immanuel Kant (1724–1804) in his *Critique of Pure Reason* was focused on answering the question of whether metaphysics as a field of philosophy was even possible and how it could be achieved.

What if the world we think is 'out there' is really just 'in here'? That is the radical position of Immanuel Kant, who put forth the theory that the principles and structures we use to interpret the world are not something out there in the world but something latent in the very form of the human mind.

Immanuel Kant.

KANT'S TRANSCENDENTAL IDEALISM

PERCEPTION OF APPEARANCES	MIND AS A TELESCOPE WITH MANY DIFFERENT FILTERS	ULTIMATE REALITY
PHENOMENAL REALM		NOUMENAL REALM

Kant's theory of transcendental idealism effected a revolution in the way we think of the world and the principles we use to understand it. In his philosophy, the mind is not a spectator of the world but an active participant helping to construct it.

Kant's theory has three major aspects. 1) The world as it actually is (metaphysical foundation of reality) is different from the world accessible to us through our senses and reason (the world as it appears to us). 2) The world accessible to us is dependent on our minds. Without our minds we would be unable to understand the world. 3) The gulf between the world as it actually is and the world as it is understandable to us is made unbridgeable by our minds. Because the mind is not some neutral tool, like a window, to simply observe the features of the world, it actively constructs the world through innate principles such as our concepts of space and time, and thereby ensures that what appears to us is different from what is out there.

Actual and Possible Worlds

You might take it for granted that only what is actual exists. Many, perhaps most philosophers, would agree with this common-sense approach. However, there are some who claim that possible worlds exist. This does not mean that a possible world could exist, but rather the more odd commitment that possible worlds exist at this very moment, right now, as possible (not possibly actual) worlds.

One such way to understand our actual world as opposed to these possible worlds is the model proposed in the second half of the 20th century by David Lewis. On his understanding, everything in the past, present and future, and everything spatially near to or far from us exists actually. This 'concrete' existence is the actual world, made of physical stuff, and possible worlds are understood in contrast to it. Importantly this does not mean that other worlds do not exist, but 'actual' here is simply meant to pick out the world which we inhabit.

Combinatorialism is a different account to make sense of possible worlds. The idea is that there are a number of elements which are the basic building blocks for any world. These metaphysical components of the world are simply rearranged differently in different possible worlds. Starting from these elements, there are increasingly complex combinations of these things which constitute the world. The most common formulation of this approach considers facts, universals and objects as most fundamental components of the world.

A more formally mathematical approach has been found in Abstractionism. In this understanding of possible worlds, a possible world is understood as a set of total

Metaphysics: pulling back the curtains of reality.

statements or properties about that world. So, the statement or property that 'you, the reader, are sitting down reading this book, while looking at these letters' is possibly true. A suitably inclusive set of propositions could be offered, at least theoretically, for the entire state of affairs in our universe where all such propositions as a set are possibly true.

Principles of Metaphysics and You

In this chapter we have surveyed some of the historically important principles of metaphysics. What can we learn from this examination? The first takeaway is that metaphysics as a field is full of principles. Whatever we make of ultimate reality will be our starting point for everything else we think about the world.

A related issue is that the use of these principles is necessary. Although metaphysical discussions often employ talk about God or a soul, metaphysical questions and more importantly, commitments, are inescapable. That is, even for those who think that matter and atoms are all that exist, this is a metaphysical belief which will inform the way you perceive and react in the world.

Lastly, metaphysics is a vast field of study with perhaps an interminable number of trivialities and speculative distractions. But this should not dissuade us from pursuing the ultimate truth about reality. Without a knowledge of where we are, it is impossible to know who we are.

**METAPHYSICS IS THE FOUNDATION UPON WHICH
PHYSICS AND EVERYTHING ELSE IS BUILT**

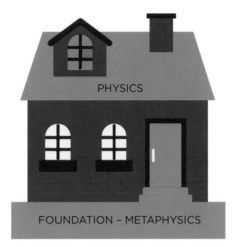

PHYSICS

FOUNDATION – METAPHYSICS

SUMMARY POINTS

- Metaphysics concerns whatever is behind the curtains of reality.
- For Aristotle metaphysics concerned the study of being, that is, things as they exist, insofar as they exist.
- The relationship of particulars to universals was articulated by Plato as a participation of individual things (particulars) imitating a Form (universal).
- Aristotle distinguished between primary substance – for example, this man right here or that horse over there – and secondary substance, the unIversal to which it belongs, the 'horse' or 'man' considered as a kind.
- Nominalism is the word used to identify those who deny, in some way, the existence of universals.
- The philosophy of René Descartes involved a sharp divide between the soul and body.
- Spinoza said there is only a single substance, God, and everything we see in the universe is a different mode of this single substance.
- The principle of sufficient reason states that everything which exists has a cause for being the way it is.
- Kant's theory of transcendental idealism placed the principles and structures of the world within the human mind.

Chapter 4

THE PRINCIPLES OF LOGIC

The discipline of logic, usually practised in academic philosophy departments, has suffered from a bad reputation. Unlike other disciplines whose very legitimacy is called into question, few doubt the truth or ability of formal logic and critical thinking. However, it comes across to the average person as a petty enterprise designed to entrap people by abstruse laws and wordplay.

Logic, many conclude, is pretentious, foreign to the way we talk and think, often inscrutable and even boring.

For those open to appreciating its complexity, there is a native elegance and beauty to the field of logic. This will come out more fully in the examples and in the history and structure of logic as we proceed. Not only is it a highly practical field but the rigorous consistency of formal logic is a model to emulate for any intellectual enterprise.

The word 'logic' derives from the Greek word *logos*. *Logos* is an immensely rich word with different meanings, but in this context it captures two elements very important to logic: 'language' and 'reason'.

Questions

How do we know that what we are saying is true? How do we formulate what we say so that it is concise? How do we evaluate someone else's argument to see if it is true? To what degree does language map on to the structure of logic?

History of the Philosophy of Logic

The formal study of logic begins with Aristotle, not because he was the first person to discuss logic but because he was the first to do so formally. Aristotle's works on logic were the basis of study for centuries and continued to be used as the standard reference up until quite recently. His entire corpus is suffused with logic at different points, but his Organon (literally 'tool') contains six works which deal for the most part directly

Aristotle.

with subjects that fit under the title of logic. Aristotle set down his analysis of logic, no doubt, in part because he wished his own thinking as well as that of others to reflect an internal consistency in a way testable by anyone who applied the principles and rules of logic.

But there was another sinister consideration motivating him. This was a cultural concern about sophists and their influence. Sophists were trained rhetoricians who taught others how to manipulate and slither their way through persuasive speeches on any topic and to any conclusion, provided the price was right.

For Aristotle, in contrast, the important issue was the form of an argument rather than its conclusion. He saw beyond the particular things being claimed in an argument, looking instead at the form or structure of the argument as a whole.

The Formal Syllogism

Aristotle's explanation of the basic form of a logical argument, the syllogism, is vague but accurate: 'With certain things being put in place, other things necessarily follow.' What he is articulating, albeit in shadow form, are the basic elements of logic: premisses and conclusion. The premisses must lead to the conclusion by a necessary rule or principle of logic, called an inference. 'Premiss' is simply a word derived from the Latin for something that has been 'sent out before'. The premisses, which are arranged a certain way because they have been 'sent out before', lead to the conclusion by a necessary and rational relationship. A premiss is itself comprised of 'terms'. A term is whatever is said or that of which something is said. For instance, 'Birds are winged animals' has two terms, 'birds' and 'winged animals'. 'Birds' is the subject, or that of which something is said, because the statement is saying of birds that they have wings. 'Winged animals' is the predicate, or what is said of the subject. Finally, Aristotle also stated that in this logical structure of syllogism it has to be clear whether something is affirmed or denied.

Here is an example of a syllogism: 1) All men are mortal. 2) Socrates is a man. 3) Therefore, Socrates is mortal. Sentences 1 and 2 are premisses. Sentence 3 is the conclusion. 'Socrates', 'man', 'men' and 'immortal' are all terms in the syllogism. Since 1 and 2 include no negations, these premisses are affirmations and not denials. The logic of the syllogism is that since all men are mortal, and Socrates is one of these men, he too must be mortal.

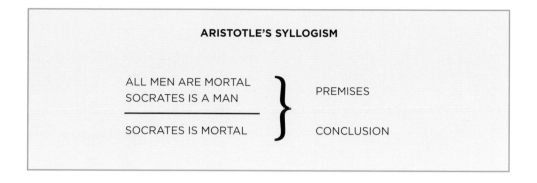

Language and Logic

I mentioned earlier the importance of language to the development of logic. As can be seen from the technical formulation of a syllogism, ensuring accuracy of the terms and claims is of the utmost importance. For Aristotle this included an analysis of the way words were being used so that we are clear on what we are saying but also so that we are not deceived by ourselves or others.

Aristotle discovered a three-fold division for the way words are applied to things. There are words that have the same name but different definitions – these are 'equivocal' words. For example, 'bank' is the same word or name when it refers to the land alongside the edge of a river and when it is applied to a financial institution. The name is the same, but the definitions differ drastically. This is the most important kind of word to be aware of, because if one definition of a word is being assumed in one premiss and a different definition in another premiss, the entire reasoning of the syllogism will turn out erroneous (termed fallacious).

The second instance of how a thing can be referred to is the 'univocal' word. A univocal word is a word for which the name and the definition are the same. Both a man and a cow can be referred to by the same word with the same definition of 'animal'.

The third type is the 'analogous' word, which is a word derived from another word. For example a 'grammarian' gains his name from 'grammar' and a 'courageous' man from 'courage'.

A frequent feature of both colloquial and formal speech is negation. We often use 'not' or 'none' or the prefix 'un-' in our negations, and Aristotle recognized that certain negative formulations can be expressed in positive ways, which may affect an argument. For example, 'possible' can be 'not impossible' or 'not necessary [that] not'.

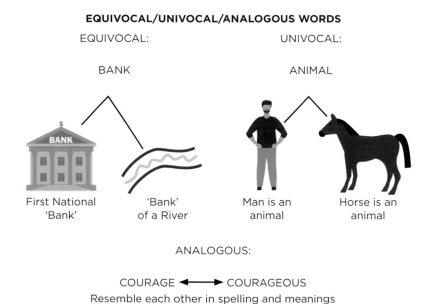

EQUIVOCAL/UNIVOCAL/ANALOGOUS WORDS

EQUIVOCAL:

UNIVOCAL:

BANK

ANIMAL

First National 'Bank'

'Bank' of a River

Man is an animal

Horse is an animal

ANALOGOUS:

COURAGE ⬌ COURAGEOUS
Resemble each other in spelling and meanings

Truth and Falsehood

Since logic is concerned with finding out the truth of things, it is no surprise that Aristotle's logic gave some consideration to the topic. Truth and falsity are not a real type of entity, but reside entirely in the mind, in thought alone. They can only be applied in cases where there is 'combination', which means that in order to be assessed for truth, a statement needs to be making a claim and connecting it, in the context of a syllogism, with other statements and claims. For instance, a prayer is neither true nor false in Aristotle's logic.

The Stoic School of Logic

Remember that for Aristotle the focus of his logic can be reduced to terms. The 'Socrates' and 'man' of the sentence 'Socrates is a man', for example. With the rise of the Stoic school of philosophy shortly after the death of Aristotle, logic began to be expanded into new directions. Instead of focusing on terms, the Stoics turned their attention to propositions.

There seem to be two distinctive reasons why their system of logic differed from that of Aristotle. The first is that they were interested in the very practical aim of refutation – of

Zeno of Citium, the founder of the Stoic school of philosophy.

proving the falsehood of certain arguments – and this concern may have been accelerated by the competitive philosophical environment at Athens, where the Stoics were competing with other philosophical schools for students and for legitimacy. The second reason, perhaps related to the first, is that the Stoics were determined to do things differently from Aristotle. This may have been because of rivalry with Aristotle, or a general theme seen in the history of philosophy: the investigative impulse to break new ground.

Just as Aristotle had, the Stoics held logic in very high esteem, granting it one of the three divisions of philosophy, along with physics and ethics. The importance of logic to philosophy can be shown in the Stoics' colourful image of logic as the skeleton of philosophy. If philosophy were an animal, ethics would be the fleshy parts, physics would be the soul, and logic would be the bones and sinews holding the whole structure together.

THE STOIC DIVISION OF PHILOSOPHY

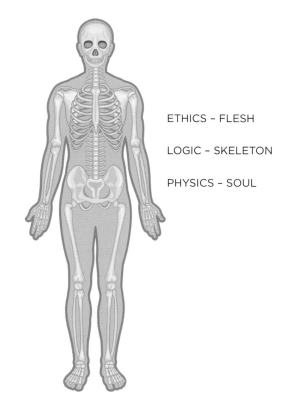

ETHICS – FLESH

LOGIC – SKELETON

PHYSICS – SOUL

THREE STOIC TERMS OF LOGIC

THING SIGNIFIED:
CONCEPT 'PILLOW'

SIGN: WORD 'PILLOW'

PILLOW

THING ITSELF
THE ACTUAL PILLOW

Logic and Language in Stoic Philosophy

The Stoics were well aware of the importance of language in constructing and assessing claims within a logical system. Logic itself had two components: rhetoric and dialectic. They taught that logic concerned a science of what is true, what is false, and what is neither.

A number of terms were commonly used by the Stoics in their formal system of logic. There are three which deserve our special attention: the 'thing signified', the 'sign' and the 'thing itself'. The thing signified is the concept which a word conjures up in our minds. So when someone says 'pillow', we have an idea of a rectangular-shaped piece of cloth filled with a soft stuffing. The sign is the sound emitted from our mouths, the pronunciation of which is a vehicle for the concept of the pillow. The last element is the thing itself: the actual physical pillow lying on the bed.

This three-fold division was also understood and explained in the context of Stoic physics, or what we would deem metaphysics. In the Stoic scheme the thing itself is physical, quite obviously, but the sign is also physical, because it is a certain portion of breath expelled from the mouth in the form of the sound of a word. The thing signified, however, is not something physical, but entirely immaterial. For this reason the Stoics said that the thing signified can be either true or false.

Porphyry's Tree

This logical 'tree' was a method of categorization made famous by Porphyry, a Platonic commentator. The logical primer this scheme was found in, the Isagoge, held sway as an introduction to logic for a millennium and a half. The tree can be visually represented as a kind of scale or tree, and it categorizes into five areas: genus, species, difference, property and accident.

The way the tree is set up is that each 'branch' splits into two options at each level, starting from the top level, which is 'being' or 'substance'. The purpose of the tree is to define what a thing is. So each successive branch adds a part of a definition. Below the top level, substance, the next two-fold division is material/immaterial. When we apply this to something and say we have a material substance, this is the definition of 'body', which will serve as the next genus in the division as substance did in the first. Body can be animate/inanimate, and if the body we are trying to define is animate, then we have arrived at the definition of a living thing, an animate, bodily substance. This process is repeated until we arrive at the complete definition of whatever we were trying to find the definition of, which might be very long. This process is only complete when no more divisions can be made.

Porphyry.

PARTIAL PORPHYRY'S TREE

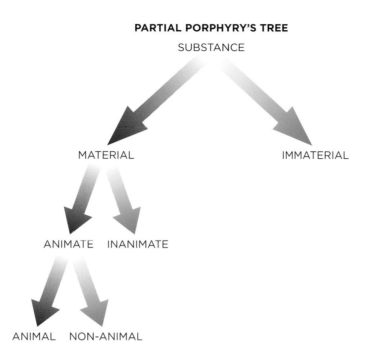

Medieval Logic

The next stop in the history of logic is necessarily brief, for – compared to the wealth of Greek sources – texts of the medieval period are lacking, although the work of Aristotle was rediscovered, leading many thinkers to propose frameworks for use in logical analysis. The subject matter of logic from the perspective of the Middle Ages is quite interesting, as it recognizes the importance of how logic is dependent on, if not wholly determined by, the human mind.

Boethius, the 13th-century theologican-philosopher who straddled the boundary between antiquity and the start of the Middle Ages, said that speech has three forms: written, spoken and mentally conceived.

There are external things out in the world which are known by the mind or soul; these would be termed 'first intentions'. Presumably examples would be what we see when we use our eyes, a green tree over here or a speeding car on the road over there. Then there are second-order thoughts, 'second intentions' in the technical vocabulary, which consider what we know about the things we encounter in the world, and begin to classify or cognize them in terms of genus, species and generally as universals of some kind. It was these second intentions that were seen as the subject matter of logic.

Boethius.

Linguistic Classifications

The relationship between language and logic was as intimate as ever. The practitioners made divisions of speech into ever more precise distinctions, aimed at aiding logical analysis. Starting with sounds, they began to situate the human voice within a sonic framework. So there are two kinds of voices: voices which are 'literate' and those which are not. Literate voices are those which can be written down in letters, while the non-literate voice cannot be. A signifying voice is an articulation of human speech which signifies or represents something to a hearer. So the word 'bed' or 'doorknob' is a signifying voice, as is the moaning of a man with a wound, since it signifies pain or distress. A part of a word such as 'pto' or a syllable such as 'la' does not signify. Signifying sounds can be natural or conventional. A naturally signifying sound is the bark of a dog or, again, the moan of a man in sickness, while conventional signifying are those sounds such as 'book' that signify an object with printed pages only by the convention associated because of the sound 'book'.

Another important distinction used in medieval logic was categorematic and syncategorematic terms. These technical but pedantic-sounding terms were meant to make the logician's job easier by placing verbs and nouns in one category, the categorematic words, while everything else in language such as adverbs and adjectives is considered syncategorematic. For our purposes, the simplest explanation is that categorematic words were applied to things which actually existed in the world, whereas syncategorematic words never signified anything existing in itself, but were best understood as helping to clarify categorematic words. For instance, in the phrase 'fish swims', fish, the noun, and swims, the verb, are categorematic. But we could also say 'every fish swims'. The word 'every' is syncategorematic in that it does not signify anything in itself and, secondly, it serves to fill out the meaning and scope of the word 'fish'.

	CATEGOREMATIC WORDS	SYNCATEGOREMATIC WORDS
TYPES OF WORDS	NOUNS + VERBS	OTHER PARTS OF SPEECH

An example sentence, with the categorematic words in bold and the syncategorematic words in italics:

The large **bird** *gladly* **flies.**

Concepts of Supposition

William of Sherwood, also in the 13th century, gave a developed theory of four different properties in logic. These are supposition, signification, copulation and appellation. Supposition is when one concept is arranged underneath another concept; it only occurs in nouns or parts of speech that sometimes have the force of a noun. Signification is the way the form or nature of something is presented to reason. Copulation is the flip side of supposition: where supposition places a concept under another, copulation puts one concept over another. Appellation is what an attribute is called when it follows a form of the verb 'is', as in 'the man is pale'.

Leibniz

The 17th century brought Leibniz, whose most significant contribution to logic was probably his theory of combinatrics. In a nutshell, this is the idea that all propositions and terms can be fundamentally turned into element units. Leibniz was influenced by what he read in the logic books of his youth, which often built up logical utterances from simpler elements to the more complex. The idea behind this is that while everything can be broken down into component parts, at some point this process has to stop, it cannot go on indefinitely. Similar to the way that an atom (or some subatomic particle) is the smallest component of matter, Leibniz believed there were smallest components of logic. Whatever these smallest components were, Leibniz considered to be the 'alphabet of human thought'.

The upshot of this process is that Leibniz could classify terms in a new way: terms are categorized based on the number of terms which comprise them. So the simplest terms are those without any components, and those with more are categorized according to the number of components they do have, in some kind of hierarchy. For example, if the alphabet consisted of only three elements, a, b and c, then the first level of the hierarchy would consist of a and b, while the second level would consist of the combinations ab, ba, ac, ca, bc, cb. The third level would consist of abc. This procedure becomes more mathematically complex as more elements are added to a basic 'alphabet', whatever those component elements turn out to be, but the essential idea is the same, that basic units of composition give rise to more complex, and that each level of combination is composed of those parts belonging to the previous level.

Mathematical Logic

As we jump to the next great period of invention in logic, the end of the 19th and into the 20th century, logicians began to formulate and conceive of logic in a way increasingly similar to mathematics. Some even understood logic to be a branch of mathematics. There were three different positions about the nature of logic: logisiticism, formalism and intuitionism.

Logisticism is the position that logic and mathematics are part of the same field, or to such a degree that it is near impossible to separate them. The reason is that logic provides the grounds for mathematical theorems, and in turn mathematical terms can be interchanged with logical terms. On this view the importance of truth was paramount. The symbols and language are not important but serve instrumentally to help get at the truths which they represent.

Formalism also granted that logic and mathematics concern the same science, but differed in thinking that the forms of mathematical and logical theorems are indeed of importance because the aim of logic is to have a consistent system of symbols free from contradiction.

Intuitionism makes the case that logic and mathematics are two separate fields. On this view, logic comes about as a result of mathematics. The consistency and patterns seen in mathematical language are abstracted and used to create a formalized logic.

Alfred Tarski

Tarski (1901–1983) was an influential logician, whose deep contributions are often only fully appreciated in philosophy departments.

One such contribution concerns the meaning of truth, and the liar paradox, which is discussed at the end of this chapter in detail. For simplification the liar paradox is best represented in the form 'This sentence is false', which, when considered, paradoxically seems to be both true and false. Part of Tarski's strategy in offering a solution was to point out that a language can mention (as oppose to use) not only a word, but entire sentences. So, for example, in English I can say that Caesar said, 'Rex vir est.' Now, 'rex vir est' has no meaning in English, since it is a Latin sentence, so it can only be mentioned (as a series of sounds or letters) and not used (to express the natural meaning of the words). So Tarski was pointing out that what the sentence 'This sentence is false' is doing is mentioning itself, but doing so without reference to its meaning, similar to the way we mentioned the Latin sentence but did not use it (assuming you can't read Latin). If it is true then, that the

Alfred Tarski.

liar's paradox involves mention and not use, it would simply be incorrect to assign a value of true or false to the sentence as a whole.

Important Principles of Logic

The Logical Square of Aristotle

The so-called square of opposition is a tool to show the relationship between different types of statements. It is necessary to refer to the diagram at the same time as this description to get a full understanding of what is going on. The basic idea is we can distil logical statements into four basic kinds: universal affirmative, universal negative, particular affirmative and particular negative. 'Universal' or 'particular' refers to the scope of the description: 'every man…' is a universal, 'Socrates' is a particular term. 'Affirmative' or 'negative' relates to whether the claim of the sentence is positive or negative. So if there is a negation of some sort, such as 'not' or 'no' as in 'No man is a mother', then the sentence is considered a negative statement.

These four different possibilities were combined into four different propositions, as mentioned above. Their schematic form can be expressed as sentences in the following way: 1) Every S is P (universal affirmative; 2) No S is P (universal negative); 3) Some S is P (particular affirmative; 4) Some S is not P (particular negative). Now each of these four propositions came to be symbolized by a single vowel as a shorthand – the universal affirmative with A, universal negative with E, particular affirmative with I, particular negative with O.

With these propositions formalized in this way, Aristotle arranged them into what has been called the square of opposition, where the relation of any two propositions is symbolized in a square. The two most significant oppositions are 'contraries' and 'contradictories'. Contraries can both be false but cannot both be true. To be a contrary,

ARISTOTLE'S LOGICAL SQUARE

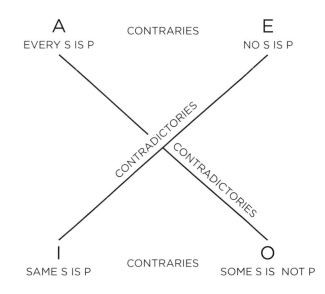

the propositions in question have to have the same subject and predicate (symbolized by 'S' and 'P') where one is a denial and one is an affirmation. A contradictory is a situation in which two propositions are opposed to each such that one of them is true while the other is false. It cannot be the case that they are both true or both false. This can be compared to the case of contraries where both propositions can be false.

The Principle of Non-Contradiction

A version of this principle can be seen as early as Plato, but its use as a fundamental element of logic occurs at all times and places. Aristotle was the first to explicitly formulate it.

This principle is a direct reflection of the square of opposition discussed above. Remember there we said that in the case of contradictories one of them has to be true, one false. This property of contradictories serves as a good indication of the nature of the principle of non-contradiction. The most straightforward formulation of this principle is

THE PRINCIPLE OF NON-CONTRADICTION

THE SAME CAR CANNOT AT THE SAME TIME BE WHITE
ALL OVER AND BLACK ALL OVER.

THE SAME CAR CAN AT THE SAME TIME BE WHITE
OUTSIDE WITH A BLACK INTERIOR.

'Something cannot at the same time and in the same respect belong and not belong to the same subject'. For example, let's take the attribute 'is good'. We cannot say at the same time that 'the car is good' and 'the car is not good'. Since these are contradictories, one of the sentences has to be true and the other false. What, however, if we say that the car is good at being gas-efficient but is not good at being low-maintenance? Wouldn't this be a case where something is both X (in this case 'good') and not X at the same time? No. The reason is that 'in the same way' is part of the principle of non-contradiction. In other words, things can be 'good' or 'expensive' or 'yellow' in one way and not in another, but never in the same way. The car can be brown (with respect to car seats) but white (with respect to the exterior paint) but it can never be brown all over and white all over.

The Principle of the Excluded Middle

This principle is closely related to what has been said about the nature of contradictories and the principle of non-contradiction. The basic idea here is a certain consequence which comes about between contradictories. Contradictories are two statements, one of them true, the other false. The principle of the excluded middle points out that there is no third option: one of these two options is true. On a practical level the principle serves to limit the logical possibilities to two.

Truth Tables

Truth tables are grids constructed to assess the truth or falsity of statements. They depend on the principle of the excluded middle in that they assume that every sentence has either a true or a false answer, and apply this analysis to complex statements, that is, statements which are themselves made up of simpler statements.

The basic idea behind a truth table is to assign the two possible truth values of true or false to every simple statement in a complex statement and, by arranging all the possible combinations of truth and falsity in these simple statements, determine the correct truth values to assign to the complex statements.

The most basic kinds of statements are affirmation/negation, either/or, both…and, and if…then conditionals. Let's take just the most basic simple sentence, negation, and see what the truth table tells us. We make a grid of two by two for a total of four squares into which we place the only four possibilities: the affirmation is true, the affirmation is false, the negation is true, the negation is false.

Note that a truth table does not determine the truth value of the simple statements, but only of the complex statements. A truth table is filled in with the numerical possibilities for the truth values of these simple statements, and these in turn give us the truth value of the complex statements.

This will be seen more clearly with one more example, this time with an either/or statement, also called a disjunction. The disjunction needs to have three columns: one for each of the two alternative terms (the 'either' and 'or' of the disjunction, which we will label 'p' and 'q') and a third one for the combination of the two terms in a complex statement. In each of the four rows we assign the possible truth values for the two terms. What we find is that the complex statement 'p or q' has a false value only when p and q are both false. Otherwise, in all the other possible scenarios, one of either p or q is true, and that's all one needs to have a true disjunction: if one of the terms is true, the disjunction is true.

TRUTH TABLE FOR A DISJUNCTION		
P	Q	P OR Q
TRUE	TRUE	TRUE
TRUE	FALSE	TRUE
FALSE	TRUE	TRUE
FALSE	FALSE	FALSE

Modalities

A word should be offered here on the topic of modalities, a great concern in modern logic. Aristotle distinguished between three different types of modalities or the way in which something is. The first way or mode is existing in the everyday manner that we are most familiar with when we we say 'The pan *is* hot' or the 'The sun *has* set'. The verbs expressed in these types of sentences are merely factual, there is nothing unusual about the conditions under which they occur. But he also distinguished 'necessary' and 'possible' modalities as well.

One of Aristotle's key insights in this regard was that these modalities are not independent of each other but are in a certain relationship. For instance, what is necessary is also what is possible. Aristotle's reasoning here is subtle, for he came to this conclusion by reasoning (through the principle of the excluded middle) that what is necessary is either possible or impossible.

When we say 'the sun is setting', this is categorized as a factual modality.

Paradoxes

Perhaps the most infamous paradox of all is the liar paradox. How exactly logic is to treat this paradox, or even categorize it, is of utmost relevance to the abilities and limitations of logic.

The most straightforward formulation of the paradox is something like 'This sentence is false'. The paradoxical nature of the sentence comes into view immediately when we ask whether it is true or false. If we say it is true, then it seems the sentence is false, for we are affirming as true what the sentence claims for itself, that it is false. If we say the sentence is false, then we are denying what the sentence claims for itself, that it is false – but by denying that the sentence is false, we make it true. So the statement is paradoxical on many levels. When we say it is true, it becomes false, and if we treat it as false, it becomes true, the opposite of what we expect. This picture of the paradox suggests to us that there is no answer. Perhaps more strongly, we feel that we have been deceived at a very fundamental level by logical method. For how can a short statement we affirm as true turn out false by the very process of affirmation?

There have been many attempts over the years to address the problems posed by the liar paradox because of the significant problems it raises for logic. Many of these are highly technical, but one proposal is that not all sentences are either true or false. Thus the liar paradox possesses a nature which cannot be evaluated on the basis of truth or falsehood.

Gödel's Incompleteness Theorem

In the 1930s Kurt Gödel put forth a theorem which had an immediate and violent impact on the mathematics and logic of the day. Bertrand Russell and A.E. Whitehead had been the latest to attempt to construct a mathematical system that was both internally consistent and complete. Gödel's theorems were aimed directly at such projects. He showed that any group of axioms proposed for a system will end up being incomplete, in the process striking a blow to the optimistic view that a purely formal logic by itself could pave the way to all philosophical knowledge.

Fallacies

The most common and most practical use of logic is in identifying fallacies (errors in/ misleading reasoning). Many of these informal fallacies, so called because they do not appeal to the form of the argument, were first documented by Aristotle in his *Sophistical Refutations*. Fallacies are a particularly clear example of how logic is tightly connected to language, for they deceive by the superficial aspect of their rhetoric, but are dissolved by examining their consistency and logic. Explicit attention to these informal fallacies has been necessary throughout the history of formal logic, as it is only after the ground has been cleared of these falsehoods that the real assessment of claims and arguments can proceed. One way of understanding what is happening in fallacies is misdirection – taking our attention away from assessing an idea in its naked form, and focusing it instead on something irrelevant to determining the truth or falsehood of the idea in question.

Despite the impression that logic may give of exhaustive systemization, there is no list of *all* informal fallacies. Rather what most logic books have on offer is a combination

Kurt Gödel.

of the most egregious and most common examples of informal fallacies. Given the elusive nature of fallacies themselves coupled with the creative use of language, the discovery of new fallacies is bound to happen.

Many of these fallacies are known by Latin names, since they were identified so long ago. Take the *post hoc ergo propter hoc* fallacy. This arises when someone assumes that because something B occurred after something A, A *caused* B. Imagine, for example, that someone thinks that because an earthquake happened during a wedding ceremony, the wedding itself caused the earthquake. Or consider the fallacy *ad populum*, which appeals to the fact that an idea or argument has been accepted by most or all people, suggesting that you too must adopt the position. An *ad baculum* fallacy, an appeal 'to the stick', is to make or even carry out a threat, as if submitting to violence makes the argument one is offering up true. 'You'd better admit that Elizabeth was the best queen, or else I will sock you in the face!' would be an example of such a fallacy. A last example of a fallacy is the *ad hominem*, which entails using insults or attacks on the character of a speaker to persuade a listener that what they say is false. An overweight gymnastics coach can in fact give good dietary advice to one of their athletes, even though they are personally physically unfit.

Principles of Logic and You

The mathematical structure and abstracted nature of logic make it a difficult subject for many. There is a sense in which our language reflects a natural logic, but most of the time it remains a substrate hidden from us under the sounds and symbols of our words. To come face to face with logic involves labour but also the uncomfortable acknowledgement that most of our thinking is not necessarily illogical but lacking the formal consistency of a logical system.

To get the most out of logic involves studying it much in the way that one performs maths problems in order to really come to an understanding of maths. What could you expect by a closer study of logic? Remember that one of the historical reasons Aristotle was led to logic was the uncovering of fallacious and misleading arguments put forth by the sophists of his day. Intentional deception by others is not the only target, however. We are also often deceived by ourselves, unwittingly and unwillingly. Logic exposes the shortcomings of our thinking and the misuse of language.

Often when people begin to study logic they quickly pick up on the enormous potential it promises in the context of arguing in personal, religious or political debates. A good deal of caution should be shown in this regard, since, although logic can tell us certain information about our arguments, it cannot tell us which arguments we should make. Just as with anything else, logic can be misused, whether by uncharitably interpreting statements made by others or by wielding logic as a pedant's hammer on the head of those without any experience in the subject. Much like language itself, logic is a tool to help us approach the truths of our ideas even if their full nature eludes us.

SUMMARY POINTS

- Logic often suffers from a reputation of being pedantic and boring, but it is a highly developed field, useful for determining truth and cultivating clarity.
- Logic comes from the Greek word *logos* which can mean both 'language' and 'reason'.
- Aristotle schematized or formalized the study of arguments by looking at the general structure instead of the particular details.
- In Aristotle's logic, truth and falsity reside only in the mind. They are not something 'in' the world.
- The Stoics made a distinction between three different terms: the thing signified, the sign and the thing itself.
- Medieval logic focused on 'second intentions', meaning the subsequent understanding we place on things when we classify them into genus, species or other universals.
- Mathematical logic concerns the attempt to understand logic in mathematical or quasi-mathematical terms.
- The principle of non-contradiction states that something cannot at the same time and in the same respect belong but also not belong to the same subject.
- Modalities are the way in which the verb of a sentence is, or is expressed, such as necessary or possible.
- The liar paradox is perhaps the paradigm case of a contradiction: whether we take the sentence 'This sentence is false' as true or false, the contradictory truth value is arrived at.

Chapter 5

THE PRINCIPLES OF ETHICS

Calendars, alarms and to-do lists are some of the most familiar tools we use to remind us of our tasks. Some people even have their weekly schedules planned out to the minute to maximize efficiency and relieve any worry about forgetting an important activity. But you can put whatever you want on a schedule – it doesn't tell you what to do, you tell it.

A calendar merely reminds you of what you already scheduled. Consider a burglar who circles Saturday night at 2 a.m. as a good time on his calendar to rob a house. There is all the difference in the world between what we *do* and what we *should* or *ought to do*.

The philosophical field in which we study what we ought to do is the field of ethics. There can be no more practical speciality in human affairs than ethics. Its aims are not only to tell us how to act and what to do but also to give an explanation for why we are to act this way.

Questions

What is the aim of life? Does the purpose of life tell me how to live? How should I act toward my fellow humans? Do I

Calendars and other tools can only tell you what you plan to do, not whether you should do that thing.

have obligations or duties to them? If there are competing systems of ethics, how do I choose between them? Do I have to be religious to be ethical?

History of the Philosophy of Ethics

In one sense the human race has always possessed a form of ethics of one kind or another. 'Ethics' as a term derives from the ancient Greek word for 'custom' or 'habit'. This is because it was thought by the ancient Greeks that the sum total of your habits shapes the way you live. Since everyone has habits, it is inescapable that everyone has some form of ethical behaviour even if they live their lives in an unreflective fashion.

Euthyphro Dilemma

It should be no surprise that ethics as a concern of philosophical study likewise goes back as far as we can find human thought. One of the more profound moral conundrums in the history of philosophy was first raised in Plato's dialogue *Euthyphro*. There the question is posed whether the holy is holy because the gods love it, or the gods love it because it is holy. The question is one of independence – are the gods independent of what is holy, or is the holy independent of the gods? This is a particularly good example for ethics because it shows how a theoretical determination has a direct impact on the actions that should be taken. In the context of the dialogue, Socrates attempts to determine what 'the holy' is. In the process he comes to assess whether the holy is independent of the gods or not, and this in turn affects what course of action he must take if he wants to act piously.

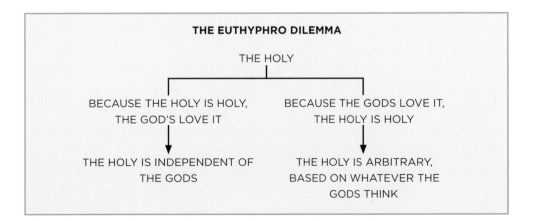

THE EUTHYPHRO DILEMMA

THE HOLY

BECAUSE THE HOLY IS HOLY, THE GOD'S LOVE IT

BECAUSE THE GODS LOVE IT, THE HOLY IS HOLY

THE HOLY IS INDEPENDENT OF THE GODS

THE HOLY IS ARBITRARY, BASED ON WHATEVER THE GODS THINK

Olympian gods.

Aristotle and Ethics

The first systematic account of ethics begins with Aristotle. As often with Aristotle, he starts at the end. He believed that the mature expression of anything was its true nature and definition, and this determined its purpose, so he begins his inquiry into ethics with a focus on happiness. For if the aim or end of human life is happiness, the goal of ethics is to determine how that happiness may be best attained.

The nature of a human is different from that of a fish or a star, so this must be taken into account to tell us how to live. In order to achieve happiness, we must factor our human nature as a rational animal into the way we behave.

Part of this was taking on board the traditional four Greek virtues of wisdom, temperance, courage and justice. In fact, Aristotle's ethical philosophy is often characterized as 'virtue ethics'. A central part of his ethical enterprise is incorporating virtues on the way to achieving happiness, because these virtues become the habits of character which help us to achieve a flourishing human life.

Aristotle divided virtues into two main categories, intellectual and ethical. Intellectual virtues consisted of wisdom, practical wisdom, scientific knowledge and virtues concerning thought. Ethical virtues included justice, self-control and human-spirited virtues such as generosity and friendship.

ARISTOTELIAN VIRTUES	
ETHICAL	INTELLECTUAL
JUSTICE	WISDOM
TEMPERANCE	PRACTICAL WISDOM
GENEROSITY	SCIENTIFIC KNOWLEDGE
FRIENDSHIP	INTELLIGENCE
WITTINESS	UNDERSTANDING
MODESTY	SENSE
MAGNIFICENCE	
MAGNANIMITY	
PROPER PRIDE	
PATIENCE	
TRUTHFULNESS	
COURAGE	

The Golden Mean

Aristotle's doctrine of the golden mean was a practical way, a general guide, of how to act ethically in a given domain by acting in accordance with virtue. The idea behind the golden mean is simple but helpful. In every area or domain of human action there is a deficient way and an excessive way to act. These are the extremes which we should avoid. Between these extremes there is a mean, and it is by this mean that virtue is achieved. For example, take the domain concerned with fear and confidence. The deficient mode of activity is to act in a cowardly fashion, while the excessive activity is to be rash. But between rashness and cowardice is courage, and that is what we should aim at.

How does the golden mean help us? There are two practical benefits to this conceptual framework. The first is that it shows how the rather abstract concept of a virtue is tied directly to a feature of our daily experience. So if we are talking about the mean for wittiness and ask ourselves how to attain such a state, it helps to contextualize what our goals are by first acknowledging this virtue occurs in the domain of conversation. Similarly, if we don't know how to be temperate, it helps to know, if nothing else, that temperance concerns the domain of pain and pleasures.

Secondly, by showing us the deficiency and excess in each domain, this approach enables us to ask ourselves, for example, whether we are being rash or cowardly in a given situation. Avoiding the extremes goes a long way toward hitting on the mean, in this case courage. Aristotle gives the helpful tip that we are often prone by nature to one of the extremes, and if this is so, we should aim at the opposite extreme, to give us a better chance of landing on the target of the mean.

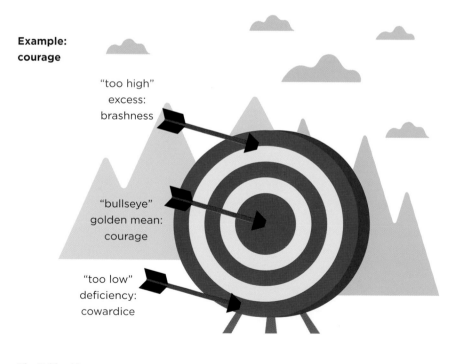

Example: courage

"too high" excess: brashness

"bullseye" golden mean: courage

"too low" deficiency: cowardice

The Golden Mean.

Stoic Ethics

The Stoics, like Aristotle, focused on virtue in their articulation of ethical theory. They elevated virtue to such a high position that they believed nothing else mattered when it came to achieving happiness besides virtue. They were so committed to this doctrine that they took the extreme view that even if someone is being tortured and in excruciating pain, as long as the man is still in possession of virtue, he is happy. Indeed, on the Stoic position, virtue is the one possession that no one is able to take away from us – presuming we have it to begin with.

Our common use of the word 'stoic' to mean someone without any emotions is historically rooted in a core truth about Stoic ethics. The Stoics sought to eliminate emotions because they believed emotions gave an importance to events or thought which they did not merit, as to have emotional responses would be an admission that we are not treating virtue as the sole object of human life and source of happiness. Since virtue alone determines how we ought to live, we should not confer the importance we reserve for it on any other aspect of our lives.

STOIC TABLE OF FALSE IMPULSES		
	GOOD	**BAD**
PRESENT	PLEASURE	PAIN
FUTURE	DESIRE	FEAR

Hedonism

Shortly after Aristotle's death, Epicureanism offered another ethical alternative. Epicurus held up pleasure as the highest and chief good. He believed that everything needed to be measured in terms of pleasure. One of the reasons he came to this conclusion is that he perceived that animals and humans, even from birth, seem to be motivated to action by pursuing pleasure and avoiding pain. Although hedonism (from the ancient Greek for 'pleasure') has earned a bad rap, the modern conception is essentially at odds with the philosophy Epicurus had in mind. He did not simply advocate an unreflective indulgence of pleasure. Instead pleasure was to be sought out with the aid of reason, and if a given path would result in pain as well as pleasure, then this should give one pause in pursuing that course of action. If a night of drunkenness leads to a hangover, then the amount of alcohol needs to be moderated so that no hangover occurs.

Epicurus.

Even if there is no drawback to pursuing a given pleasure, abstemiousness and moderation should be used in deciding when to indulge. For instance, Epicurus pointed out that by abstaining from food and bread for a time, this makes the food and bread more pleasurable when it is consumed. This insight rested on one of Epicurus' somewhat controversial ideas, that pleasure could never be increased beyond a certain threshold. It could be changed in type, but it could never be augmented in degree. An addict, Epicurus would say, is someone who does not recognize that there is a limit to the pleasure he has – he cannot simply go on adding to it, but must either take a break or alter the source from which he derives pleasure.

Immanuel Kant

To leap now from ancient Greece to the 18th century and the Enlightenment, the thinking of Immanuel Kant is often considered a Copernican revolution in philosophy. In addition to his contributions in other philosophical fields, Kant brought the concept of duty to the forefront of his ethical theory. The great term for 'what must be done' *'deon'* was adopted for this theory of ethics. Deontology is the study of what ought to be done, the focus on duty as of prime ethical importance.

Kant proposed what he termed the 'categorical imperative', which took several formulations. 'One ought not to treat other persons as a means, but only as ends in themselves.' Another version of it reads that we should act only in that way which we wish to make a universal law. What does the categorical imperative require then? It is universal in scope and requires that we treat every human as an individual. Furthermore, the way we act should serve as a paradigm for all further moral actions of the same kind – if we do not wish a given action to be a standard for conduct then we have lost sight of the aim of the categorical imperative.

We should examine for a moment how Kant contrasts the categorical imperative with his hypothetical imperative. A categorical imperative applies to all times and places, whereas a hypothetical imperative is limited to a specific circumstance. The hypothetical is so named because it only has one goal in mind, and that specific aim is furthered by the hypothetical imperative, as opposed to the categorical imperative which is more universal.

Let us take, for instance, a situation in which an elderly woman is having difficulty crossing the street. Following the categorical imperative, we would treat the woman as an end in herself rather than, say, as merely an inconvenience, and therefore we would help her cross the street. But let's say that the same situation comes about but in this instance

IMPERATIVES IN KANT

THE HYPOTHETICAL IMPERATIVE

ACTION DETERMINED BY
PREFERENCE AND GOAL

THE CATEGORICAL IMPERATIVE

ACTION DETERMINED BY DUTY

EXAMPLE: IF I WANT TO
CHOP WOOD, THE OBJECT
I USE MUST BE HARD AND SHARP.

EXAMPLE: I MUST NOT LIE
TO THIS MAN.

you see your work boss standing on the other side of the road. You take note of this and think to yourself, 'My boss will be impressed by my philanthropic spirit if she sees me helping grandma across the street.' Under these conditions you have fulfilled a hypothetical imperative. The mental hypothetical you processed in your head was something like, 'If I help this woman cross the street, my boss will be impressed.' This can be expressed more explicitly as, 'Given that I want to be promoted at work, I should perform this action to impress my boss.' This is a prudential reason, and it happens to coincide with self-interest, although it need not. The relevant difference from the categorical imperative is that the particular goals of a particular individual in a hypothetical imperative can never be universalized. Think of how absurd it would be to think that everyone is motivated to act so as to impress their boss. What about those who are the boss, or do not have one, or who want to get fired? Such a motivation would never appeal to them.

Utilitarianism

Utilitarianism is a system of selecting the correct course of action by finding the greatest good, or the greatest happiness. The greatest good, as we will see, is a notoriously difficult thing to discover, and it is both a benefit and a drawback to the system that it is broadly defined. While Kant brought personal duty to the forefront, utilitarianism sought to elevate the needs of others and the needs of everyone.

Jeremy Bentham (1748–1832) was the philosopher who first advocated utilitarianism as a system. He measured utility by whatever produces 'benefit, advantage, pleasure, good or happiness' or prevents the opposite of these states and circumstances. A good course of action or, more generally, a good system of ethical guidance is one which maximizes the benefits and advantages and lessens the drawbacks and disadvantages for as many people as possible.

Helping an old woman across the street.

Jeremy Bentham.

John Stuart Mill.

In Bentham's conception, pleasure was so closely tied to happiness that the measure which he used to tabulate the maximization of happiness was called the 'hedonic calculus'. His student, the polymath John Stuart Mill, later brought utilitarianism a higher level of both notoriety and legitimacy.

There have been different variations of the utilitarian ethic. Act utilitarianism focuses on individual action and asks us to determine, one act at a time, whether it will tend to maximize happiness. Rule utilitarianism instead advocates adoption of that course of action, generally followed, that would tend to promote the greatest happiness.

Objections to Utilitarianism

Perhaps the most strident and persuasive arguments against utilitarianism stem from what appears to be its necessary antagonism with human rights. If what we ought to do is concerned wholly with maximizing the overall good, then this requires we sometimes trample over the rights of individuals so that the good of the majority is maximized. This could involve the confiscation of private property or organ harvesting from those who are deemed to not have enough utility, such as the elderly or the homeless. On a more fanciful note, it would also appear to force those who are extraordinarily gifted to only engage in the kind of profession which would lead to benefits for the whole of society, even if it created misery in that person's life.

Consequentialism

Do the ends justify the means? In some sense, an affirmative answer to this question is at the heart of consequentialist ethical theory. Consequentialism, as the name implies, looks at the consequences of an action to determine whether it is ethically recommendable or not. As you can tell, utilitarianism is consequentialist since it assesses the consequences of actions, in terms of whether they lead to the increase of happiness and pleasure. However, consequentialism is a broader ethical theory than utilitarianism. Utilitarianism is but one kind of consequentialism.

We might think looking to the *consequences* gives a straightforward metric by which to judge our actions. But consequences can be measured in different ways and this determines the type of consequentialism.

A more unusual and perhaps unsettling form of consequentialism is act egoism. Under this theory someone pursues those activities which maximize their own interests, defined in terms of consequences. This view might seem to be repugnant at first glance, since it downplays the interests of others, but it is often moderated so it is not so much that other people do not count, but more an acknowledgement their concerns are not weighted as heavily as our own self-interest. Act egoism is an agent-centred ethical theory since it focuses primarily on the individual.

TWO KINDS OF CONSEQUENTIALISM	
UTILITARIANISM	**ACT EGOISM**
ACT TO MAXIMIZE HAPPINESS	ACT TO MAXIMIZE PERSONAL GAIN

By contrast, we can distinguish agent-neutral forms of consequentialism. Under this heading would fall the varieties of utilitarianism, since they incorporate the needs and concerns of all, in a way that is neutral to the agent who performs them – there is no special consideration afforded to the agent.

Rule consequentialism is another theory which is conceived in agent-neutral terms. In rule consequentialism those rules are to be followed which generally result in the best consequences for everyone.

The central problem for this theory is how to determine the consequences, when the complexities of the world often make it difficult to know how things will turn out. So the tension to be resolved is whether the consequences we should aim for are the actual consequences or the anticipated consequences of our actions, two categories which only sometimes align.

Important Principles of Philosophy

Good and Evil

At its most basic level, the field of ethics is considered by many to concern the distinction between good and evil, and how we may apply this distinction to identify the good which we ought to pursue while shunning the evil. Ethics, on this view, is almost like going on a walk so that we can point out what things are good and bad. This conception of ethics is often totalizing: everything and everyone is tabulated into the two columns of good and evil. It furthermore raises the unreasonable expectation that distinguishing the good from the bad is always a clear and easy matter.

At the beginning of his book *Beyond Good and Evil*, Friedrich Nietzsche (1844–1900) traces the problematic aspects of both Christianity and the philosophical school of Plato to the central importance they grant to

Friedrich Nietzsche.

the concept of good and evil. The merits of Nietzsche's critique aside, his attack rightly identifies how good and evil serve as the foundation for ethical thinking, whether religious or philosophical.

At the same time as there is a primordial acknowledgement of evil, there is also an inadequate groping to define it adequately. Some philosophers have characterized what is evil as that which is undesirable in itself. This seems to be overly broad and perhaps liable to the charge that people's desires are fickle and often inadequately informed. Another line of thought is that evil is an unmerited harm committed against certain kinds of living things, perhaps sentient or moral animals, and the harm has to reach some minimum threshold. This understanding of evil centres on anthropology – that is, it is an understanding of evil necessarily linked to human experience. The Platonist philosopher Plotinus a few hundred years into the modern era, by contrast, defined evil simply as the lack of the good. By doing so, he denied that evil has a robust existence, or indeed any existence at all: it is completely parasitic on the existence of the good.

Non-Cognitivism

It may seem a strange idea, but there is an entire stream of philosophy that views ethical claims as nothing more than mushy feelings. This is the position of the non-cognitivist, who believes that moral statements or beliefs purport to say something about the world, but in fact are only expressions about the preferences of those who have these beliefs. Another way of stating this is that moral statements cannot be evaluated in terms of true or false, because there simply is no way to evaluate them, to check them, to see how they could be true. To what can one turn to confirm the idea that 'theft is evil'? The non-cognitivist appeals to the fact that our moral statements appear to be grounded in something quite mysterious or nothing at all. To be sure, this position is sceptical and reductive, and its origin is the

Plotinus.

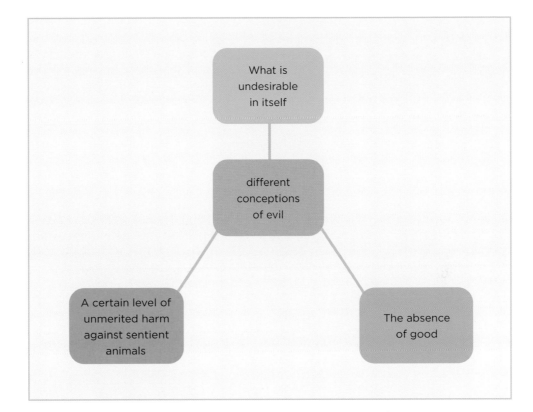

idea that everything that is true or false needs to be assessable empirically. On this account, moral judgements amount to nothing more than mental mumbo jumbo giving us a glimpse at the aspirations and prejudices of the would-be moralizer, but do not tell us anything about the truth. 'That man is bad', for instance, would translate for the non-cognitivist into something like 'I do not like that man' or 'He did something I disapprove of'.

Conscience

Arguably the first source and first experience of our ethical lives can be categorized as the experience of the conscience. The conscience has been criticized as lacking the precision and consistency of more formalized ethical thought, but what it lacks in exactitude, it more than makes up for in terms of conviction and authority. For this reason conscience has often been considered the most powerful goad for ethical activity. Some, including Sigmund Freud, have seen in the ancient Greek figures of the Furies a

The Three Furies.

personification of the conscience. These ghoulish avenging spirits would hound guilty individuals until the due penalty was paid.

Nevertheless it is difficult to precisely trace the conscience as a philosophically laden concept, and the word itself is a fairly recent development. Its Latin root suggests conscience is a kind of knowledge of oneself, or perhaps an accessory special feature that comes along with knowledge – some faculty which pronounces judgement on the knowledge we already possess.

As a moral principle some have granted the conscience a special privilege. If an action goes against it, the conscience should be inviolable. We should never violate our conscience, and as a result, a second-order consequence is derived as well: that we should also never violate the conscience of someone else.

The nature of the conscience is fundamental to assessing its worth and authority as a source of ethical guidance. Does the conscience work in the realm of knowledge, or does its guidance stem from a source entirely non-rational, like an instinct spurring us in a certain direction? Is it ever the case that the conscience dictates actions to us that are in conflict with reason? If that happens, does it indicate to us that the conscience is unreliable on a more general level?

The distinguishing mark of the conscience is not merely that it informs or reveals the correct action, for this could come by other means, such as rationality. The very fact that the conscience sometimes arrives at different conclusions from our rational calculations tells us that it is *something* different from reason. So we do not merely pronounce whatever decisions we arrive at to be 'our conscience'. Rather the conscience is a different source of practical guidance entirely, whether it is a special form of knowledge or merely intuition baptized with legitimacy.

This raises the question of whether the conscience as an ethical principle requires us to admit that it is a form of moral relativism. The most suggestive reason to think so is that if moral activity is ultimately reliant on the deliverances of our conscience, then surely consciences differ among themselves as to background knowledge, judgement, wisdom and so forth. At the very least this would suggest that consciences are dependent to a large degree on the individuals who possess them, and that they can be at odds. John says the atomic bombs dropped on Japan in 1945 were moral and Jane denies this, while both appeal to their conscience.

Perhaps then, we want to grant the conscience a place at the table in our moral calculation, as an indication of sincerity and of coherent conviction, but not grant it a wholly autonomous or privileged role in our decision making.

The mushroom cloud over Nagasaki after the atomic bomb was dropped.

Habit

Habit is of extreme importance in all conceptions of ethics, none perhaps more so than in Aristotle's theory of virtue. The root of the word ethics, in ancient Greek, means to be accustomed to do something, or to usually do something. This not only implies a degree of consistency to whatever it is that is done, but also suggests a point so obvious as to be taken for granted, that habit is an activity. Habit is a consistent activity, and this in turn not only was thought, at least by the ancient Greeks and Romans, to form one's character but was also identified with character itself.

One reason to aim for this inculcation of habit is to arrive at a state of ethical development which is second nature. Consider a farmer who has been waking up at 4.00 in the morning since he was a child. To the sluggish urbanite, waking up at such an hour seems to be not only a punishment but a biological impossibility. To the farmer, however, who has fashioned his character over a long period into someone who rises before the sun, there is nothing special about his waking habits. So ingrained is his habit that he does not need an alarm clock, because through long practice rising at 4 a.m. has become second nature to him.

At any rate, the formation of habit is an important activity of ethical life. We usually think of ethics as necessarily involving conscious choice, so that circumstances with difficult choices represent the epitome of the moral life. Habits, however, are ingrained patterns of behaviour which have long ceased to be thought about; their tenure in an individual human psyche has been so long that conscious choice is no longer a relevant description.

Punishment

The topic of important principles in ethics could hardly be broached without discussing punishment. While we do not necessarily think that proper ethical behaviour necessitates an immediate and proportionate reward, many share the conviction that moral transgression calls forth and requires punishment.

But what is punishment? When is punishment justified and why do we feel the draw to punish? These are some of the important questions revolving around the ethical call for punishment.

In the 17th century Thomas Hobbes considered punishment the infliction of pain, while more recent attempts to capture the idea have relied on the core notion of deprivation. There are practical matters to clear up as well, such as who should adjudicate and enforce the punishment, and to what degree this process is essential to the definition of justice.

Although the aforementioned considerations are difficult, the most serious problem with the definition of punishment is that in attempting to clarify the concept, we craft the definition such that it conforms to what we want punishment to accomplish. This is a liability for whatever ethical theory we use.

Retributionist View of Punishment

The traditional view of punishment has been called the retributionist view. For the retributionist, punishment is almost like an ethical version of Newton's law that for every action there is an equal and opposite reaction. For serious ethical and legal transgressions there is an equal punishment which must be doled out. This punishment is considered the 'just deserts' of the offender, and it is a feature of justice that they merit and must be made subject to a certain punishment for their crime. The retributivist impulse usually brings with it the conviction that the offender must pay the penalty. This is another way of saying that other considerations, such as the circumstances under which the offender committed the transgression or expectations of personal reform, are either ignored altogether or downplayed.

Central to the conception of just deserts is the Latin phrase 'lex talionis'. This translates to something like 'the law of so much', and the idea is that whatever crime is committed ought to be punished with a punishment of equal kind and degree. Some conceptions of this dictum require that the punishment fit the crime exactly, so that if the criminal performed crime X, he should be punished with that same action applied to himself. If he stole money, he should have money taken from him, or if he kidnapped someone, then he should be taken and imprisoned against his will.

Often the retributionist theory is associated with the idea of deterrence. If punishment is swift, proportionate and enacted directly on the transgressor, this is thought to be a check against future infractions by the same person. In a general way punishment is also thought to act as a deterrent for the public at large.

Other theories of punishment take other considerations as factors, often multiple factors at once, such as the rights of the offenders, the impact on the offender's future life and present family, and the opportunity for a 'second chance'. Sometimes these notions fall under the heading of restorative justice. More recently, focus has been shifted to equity, so that historically marginalized groups are relieved from the burden of punishment.

TWO DIFFERENT FORMS OF PUNISHMENT		
	RETRIBUTIVE JUSTICE	**RESTORATIVE JUSTICE**
AIM	'JUST DESERTS' FROM OFFENDER	RECONCILIATION OF OFFENDER
MAIN BENEFIT	PUNISHMENT FITS CRIME	CRIMINAL IS REFORMED

Moral Realism vs Moral Relativism

We met the notion of moral relativism in discussing conscience. Even most non-philosophers have a conception of relativism, more or less meaning that there is no actual right or wrong, only differing personal conceptions of right and wrong. Moral realism, by contrast, says that moral qualities are real. It really is bad to steal or wicked to murder someone.

Moral relativism is in one sense an easy refuge for those who do not want to commit to an ethical system but fear inviting criticism or perhaps charges of inconsistency. On the other hand moral relativism abolishes the aim of ethics as a field. Presumably we want to find out what the right thing to do is in some general and very important sense, an objective standard which stands outside of our own judgement and preference. If there are no moral laws, how could I criticize someone else for stealing my car? If moral relativism is true, stealing my car might be good for the thief, and who am I to call into question his actions – given that all morality is relative?

Moral Realism vs Non-Cognitivism

Another angle to better understand the claims of moral realism is to contrast it with the awkwardly named 'non-cognitivism' (see above). Non-cognitivism advances the claim that ethical judgements and states are not about what is true or false; they do not represent reality, but are expressive of an emotional state or something similar. The important takeaway is that according to the non-cognitivist perspective, ethical pronouncements are not analogous to 'seeing' things as they are in the world but rather they impose meaning where there is none. Ethical and moral statements do not express facts.

One way the non-cognitivist thesis is expressed is that when there is a conflict of ethical consequence between two parties, this is really nothing more than a fight over feelings. The moral realist would say that two people disagreeing over whether it is wrong to steal have a dispute about whether stealing is 'right or wrong'. For the non-cognitivist, in contrast, the language of 'stealing is wrong' masks the underlying conviction, which might be something like 'stealing is unpleasant to me' or 'stealing is not of any use to modern man'. In the non-cognitivist world, there are no moral facts, because moral or ethical statements are to be translated into a different framework in order to be understood.

NON-COGNITIVISM

MAN STEALING A CAR

Stealing a car is evil

You really mean 'This theft is undesirable to me'

Traditional moralist   Non-cognitivist

Rights

Many of the contentious political issues of our day are discussed in terms of a right of one kind or another. There is something absolute and binding about the possession of a right, as it confers upon someone a power to exercise that right free from the interference of others – whether it is the right to vote or speak or even be free from torture.

Although rights, especially human rights, are a common feature of contemporary discourse, their foundation or the grounds upon which they are justified have often been obscured. This owes in part to the fact that rights often arise as laws conferred through convention, though the reality which we assume they reflect is something beyond the civil formalization. That is, we think a right is something that necessarily belongs to someone, whether as a human, a citizen or some other status. The concept of a right also seems to have a relationship to duties and obligations – a right is something that grants one the ability to execute them. Take, for example, the right to vote. It is not only the case that one has the right to vote, but there is a presumption that fulfilling the duty to vote benefits one's fellow citizens. It is proper to exercise the right because, in so doing, it is good for all.

Eleanor Roosevelt and the universal declaration of human rights.

It may appear to us that rights as a philosophical concept are compatible with many different ethical theories. That may be true, but it is also the case that there are rights-based ethical theories. The basic idea is that there are fundamental ethical rights we have by virtue of being ethical agents. In turn these rights should be acknowledged by others and possibly even enshrined in law. Furthermore, no hindrances should be introduced to the exercise of these rights, legally or otherwise.

Principles of Ethics and You

There are many ethical systems and many ethical theories. In fact, there are so many that this chapter cannot contain them all. Many share overlapping concerns and goals, but there are also overt antagonistic elements between them, such as utilitarianism and the virtue-dominated system of Stoicism. Nevertheless, this should not be an invitation to despair at identifying ethical behaviour. I hope that by exposing you to the varieties of ethical theorizing this will open you up to the vast complexities of ethical situations. Some matters are quite simple. It is good not to steal and it is bad to murder. But this leaves open an entire field of ethical opportunities not captured by these rather simple and obvious moral choices. The two most relevant instances are our life as a whole, considered from the position of someone who wishes to lead a conscientious life in the long term, and the more difficult decisions which often involve conflicting values or uncertain, complex circumstances. It is in these situations that we ought to turn to ethical theories which can serve, if not as outright guides, at least as clarificatory principles to help us in a situation where we would otherwise be completely blind.

SUMMARY POINTS

- 'Ethics' comes from the Greek for 'custom' or 'habit' and so concerns actions.
- Aristotle defines the proper activities of mankind as whatever leads to the achievement of happiness.
- Stoic ethics took virtue to be the chief, and as it turned out, the only good.
- Hedonism is guided by the principle of pleasure.
- Immanuel Kant formulated the categorial imperative, a duty which honoured the rational moral agency of human beings.
- Utilitarianism is a philosophy pursuing actions that benefit the greatest number of people, often characterized as the greatest good and greatest happiness.
- The distinction between good and evil lies at the heart of ethical discussion.
- Common philosophical conceptions of evil range from the psychological (that which is undesirable) to the quasi-legal (an unmerited harm against other humans) to the metaphysical (evil is the lack or privation of what is good).
- The belief that there is no right or wrong but only differing conceptions of right and wrong is moral relativism.
- Non-cognitivism is the philosophical theory that ethical statements are subjective emotional judgements clothed in ethical disapproval.

THE PRINCIPLES OF LANGUAGE

Ludwig Wittgenstein said that the goal of philosophy is to help us escape from the bewitchment of language. He also cryptically announced, 'philosophical problems arise when language goes on holiday.' Whatever we make of these remarks, Wittgenstein (1889–1951) recognized that philosophy and language have a long and intimate relationship.

The history of philosophy is an enterprise concerned with the precise use of words, the articulation of what borders the inexpressible, and a focus on the paradoxical and puzzling problems that arise in linguistic form. Whether these philosophical enquiries occur in the medium of language and so are essentially beyond language, or philosophy, in some fundamental sense, merely is language, is part of the problem which Wittgenstein's remark raises.

Even in some of the central features of philosophy it can be difficult to determine whether or not language itself is the subject matter at hand or something else. 'What is it?' Socrates used to frequently ask, and the answer he sought was a definition. 'What do you mean?' we often ask, and separating out the 'meaning' of the answer we receive is often impossibly inseparable from the language it is expressed in. Many poets, historians, writers and others whose work primarily involves the mastery of words have been uninterested in the intricacies of philosophy. But it is impossible for a philosopher to avoid engaging with language and words, and being drawn into a world of overwhelming fascination.

Ludwig Wittgenstein.

Questions

What is language? How do we get from language to meaning? Is philosophy nothing more than word wrangling? Is it possible to get beyond language, to access knowledge or truth either through language or despite it? What are the capabilities and limits of language, and do these determine the way we understand everything?

History of Philosophy of Language

Plato

Language, and so the philosophy of language, goes very far back into the history of the human race. Plato considered Homer a philosopher, and often invokes the words found in the *Iliad* and *Odyssey* as sound advice. Central to Plato's approach to language was etymologizing the origin of words. Some modern commentators think that Plato's etymologizing speculations were spurious or entirely indulgent, but it is clear that Plato granted language, even at the minute level of words, a special relationship to reality. This relationship would be explored and brought into question again and again through the history of philosophy.

Plato wrote an entire dialogue, *Cratylus*, on the topic of language. A central part of the discussion is whether language is just a convention or whether there is some deeper connection between words and the way things are. The position that words are conventions is in direct opposition to the idea that words reveal deep realities.

The conventionalist argument in the *Cratylus* makes the claim that things have names simply by the repeated association of a name with that thing. If people had assigned a different name to it, then we would call the thing by that name. If enough people call a rose a 'peanut', then by the convention of use, over time 'peanut' will become the correct

A scene from the Iliad.

designation for what we now call a 'rose'. In fact one of the characters in the dialogue even goes so far as to suggest that if everyone else calls something by one name, and someone else has his own private name for the same object, then the object has two names. Against this view is the contention that there is only one right name for every thing. At this point, we might not be swayed by either side, but if we pause for a moment, this is a great insight in the history of examining language philosophically.

CONVENTIONALISM VS NON-CONVENTIONALISM

NAMES *ARE* A CONVENTION: WE CAN CALL THIS A 'PEANUT'

NAMES ARE *NOT* A CONVENTION; 'ROSE' REFLECTS THE REALITY OF WHAT THIS FLOWER IS

Plato separated out what is so difficult for many: the word from the thing signified by the word. But it is only once this relationship has been uncovered that the more important work begins. For as soon as we see a division between reality and words we must next determine whether the relationship between the two is one of similarity or difference. If we think words bear no relationship to the reality they represent, then words and things are fundamentally different – words are conventions.

Aristotle

Aristotle's contributions to the philosophy of language are immense, and some of his many ideas can be found in the chapter on logic, the whole field of which can be understood as an attempt to clarify and formalize language. Here, however, we will turn to his analysis of the ways in which language can be used to confuse and deceive, intentionally or not. In his work *On Sophistical Refutations* Aristotle offers several insights into this distinction between words and the things they represent. He is primarily interested in the use of arguments and the occasions when they are fallacious, so he explains that words can function much like appearances. For example, tin can shimmer and appear to be silver in the right circumstances, and language can function in this deceptive manner as well. The tools of philosophy help us to uncover this deceit. Another analogy, taken from mathematics, also shows why it is easy to be deceived. Imagine you are counting using little pebbles to mark the advance of your numbering, '45, 46, 47…'. Aristotle says that we come to associate the thing we use to count with the number itself (rather than merely to track or signify the number), and we are in danger of doing the same thing with language – mistaking words for the things they signify.

WORDS AS SIGNS

USING PEBBLES AS PLACEHOLDERS FOR NUMBERS

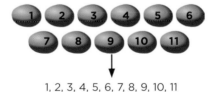

1, 2, 3, 4, 5, 6, 7, 8, 9, 10, 11

IS THE SAME AS USING WORDS AS PLACEHOLDERS FOR MEANING

'THIS SENTENCE IS ONLY A SIGN –
THE LETTERS OR THE SOUNDS OF
THE SENTENCE ARE ONLY SYMBOLS
TO CONVEY THE MEANING'

MEANING

Getting the relationship right between words and the deeper realities they point to is of fundamental importance to Aristotle. Language must be set aright by philosophical analysis so that it matches up with what it can and should say. Take equivocation, the fallacy which makes use of two different meanings of the same word to make an argument. 'Nothing matters more than love. Love matters more than everything. Therefore nothing matters more than everything.' In this argument the meaning of 'nothing' in the first sentence is not treated as a real substance as it is in the third sentence. It is an equivocation and the syllogism (this type of reasoning from two premises) is false. Another situation is ambiguity, where a word or sentence can have multiple meanings. One of the examples Aristotle offers is 'Of the silent to speak it is possible'. This sentence can mean that it is possible to talk about those who are silent. But it can also take on the contradictory meaning that it is possible for the silent to speak (while they remain silent).

The Fallacy of Equivocation

A) **Nothing** matters more than love

B) Love matters more than everything

C) Therefore, *nothing* matters more than everything

Nothing in bold means 'there is not a thing'.

Nothing in italics means 'non-existence'.

Since the meaning of 'nothing' differs in A and C, the conclusion is false.

After going through these and other fallacies, Aristotle says that he is going to talk about fallacies not dependent on language. So as a matter of philosophical method in the case of language, he seems to believe that it is necessary to first clear away the mistakes we make with language before proceeding to investigate other, more substantial errors.

Already in what we have seen, there is a great deal of overlap between language and logic. The previous chapter on logic has covered much of the Stoic and medieval theories about language by relating their thoughts on logic. So, to avoid overlap with that chapter, we will press forward to the modern era of the philosophy of language, the age in which language increasingly became a focus of philosophers in the change of approach known as the 'linguistic turn'. However, in passing it is worth noting the influence of Aristotle on medieval academia. In the 12th and 13th centuries the study and spread of Aristotle lead to treating language as another field of philosophical enquiry. This vigorous analysis, in the hands of the so-called 'speculative grammarians', became so theoretical that it led to a neglect of the classical Latin literary authors as all the intellectual focus shifted to this new study of grammar.

Francis Bacon

Bacon (1561–1626) wrote a work called the *New Organon*. Aristotle's work on language and logic had been called the *Organon*, meaning 'tool', so Bacon consciously was weighing in on what he deemed to be Aristotle's old and obsolete method. In Bacon's view Aristotle relied upon the syllogism too much, for it could do no more than organize knowledge we already possessed through deduction. Instead Bacon championed the idea of induction, or the possibility of new knowledge.

One of the central problems identified by Bacon was the origin and use of language. Language arose as a way for people to communicate with each other about everyday life. It is not naturally equipped for the precision and loftiness needed for science or philosophy. The nature of language is such that it is does not actually touch reality the way Aristotle or medievalists conceived of it. On the contrary, words always rely on other words for their meanings and definition. Furthermore, in a striking metaphor, Bacon said that words influence our thoughts very strongly – they 'shoot back' like a bow when it releases an

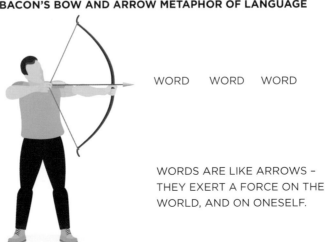

BACON'S BOW AND ARROW METAPHOR OF LANGUAGE

WORD   WORD   WORD

WORDS ARE LIKE ARROWS –
THEY EXERT A FORCE ON THE
WORLD, AND ON ONESELF.

arrow. Words affect us even as we use them, and this influence, in Bacon's view, is not always good. One of the practical results of this thinking was that Bacon minimally relied on language for his scientific explorations, instead preferring to lend weight to empirical investigations.

Thomas Hobbes

Hobbes (1588–1679) was similarly suspicious of the power of language when it came to knowledge. However, there was one area in which he granted considerable importance to words. Hobbes said that the concept of universals – for example, a property or category – is impossible for the human mind to grasp except by language. At least on this single issue, language has been granted a special role in allowing us to see from a vantage we would not be able to enjoy without it. There are only individual things in the world, according to the Hobbesian view, but our language combines and yokes them together in different ways.

René Descartes

Descartes (1596–1650) has been infamous in the history of philosophy for discounting animals, specifically denying they have souls. One reason he believed this was that they possess no language in the way humans do. So, unlike Bacon and Hobbes, Descartes had a high view of language, believing this capacity was central to human reasoning.

One thing that Descartes proposed was that it was possible for humans to attain to a universal language. What he meant by this is that language is reducible to a certain set of finite ideas, and these ideas in combination can be used to form a precise, universal language. This contrasts with the belief that language itself structures our thought, and so each language is necessarily partitioned off from all the others, and it also is at odds with the hypothesis that non-linguistic influences, such as our temperament or bodily constitution, are what determine our thoughts.

Gottfried Leibniz

Leibniz (1646–1716) granted that language has a relationship to the realities in the world. But he moderated this commitment by acknowledging that this need not require exactitude. Words can be approximations of the realities they represent. They can achieve fidelity without attaining perfection. An analogy is that a model train can represent a full-size coal train, without showing every last detail or containing every

LEIBNIZ'S MODEL OF LANGUAGE

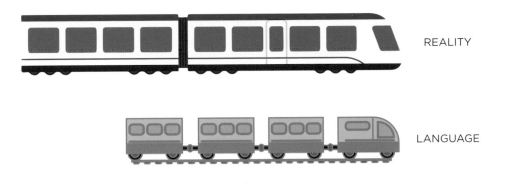

REALITY

LANGUAGE

JUST AS A MODEL TRAIN CAN ACCURATELY, BUT WITH LIMITATIONS,
MODEL A FULL-SIZED TRAIN, SO LANGUAGE CAN MODEL THE WORLD.

mechanical structure; it can still give us a very good idea of what a working coal train looked like in the late 1800s, even if we have never seen one before.

By positing this analogous structure of language and knowledge, Leibniz made room for a relationship between different languages. If language A and language B both understand concept X, but in different ways according to their own structures, Leibniz's theory says that A and B will resemble each other in a certain way. Thus there is a common, logical element which all languages share.

Gottlob Frege

Frege (1848–1925) is a figure central to modern philosophy's shift in relation to both logic and language. In the phenomenon of language Frege saw the vehicle of thought: it was only through this medium that any thoughts could be had. Thus he sought a rigorous and precise language suitable for the serious work of philosophy.

He proposed several concepts influential in the philosophy of language, the first of which is called the context principle. This is the idea that a word is never separable from the context in which it appears, normally the sentence or even a larger unit of text.

Frege also proposed an interesting theory of language in an attempt to make logic independent of the mind. Previous philosophers had tried to say that logic is an attempt to formulate human thought. This sounds unobjectionable, but it makes it appear that the nature of logic can change if human thoughts change and, perhaps more alarmingly, if there were no human thought, there would be no logic. Frege posited that thoughts were not something entirely private but were publicly shared. This meant they have an independent existence outside of individual minds. Frege did not deny that there were

Gottlob Frege.

some personal and even idiosyncratic elements in the way people think, but he said that these features were not relevant to the thought of a sentence. In making this move, Frege positioned logic as something real and existing outside the mind or, at the very least, outside the mind of individuals.

Sense and Reference

An article which Frege published in 1892 had an enormous influence on 20th-century philosophy of language. In 'Sense and Reference' he distinguishes between the two terms sense and reference. Reference is a rather easy concept: it simply means the real object in the world to which a name refers. So if I say Fred, I refer by this name to the actual person Fred sitting at the desk in the library across from me. In order to understand the idea of sense, however, it will be much easier if we think of an example from superhero mythology: Clark Kent and Superman.

Pretend you are Lex Luthor, mortal enemy of Superman and genius. Now imagine one of your henchmen informs you that 'Clark Kent is Clark Kent', while another henchman arrives at the same time and tells you 'Clark Kent is Superman'. You dismiss the first numbskull henchman, for he has told you something both you and everyone

SENSE AND REFERENCE

BOTH 'CLARK KENT' AND 'SUPERMAN' HAVE THE SAME REFERENCE, THE SON OF JOR-EL, THE KRYPTONIAN. BUT THEIR SENSE, OR MODE OF PRESENTATION, DIFFERS.

HENCHMAN A — Clark Kent is Clark Kent

HENCHMAN B — Clark Kent is Superman

LEX LUTHOR — Henchman B has really told me something useful.

else already know. Of course Clark Kent is Clark Kent. But on the other hand, your competent henchman has really given you an important piece of information. 'Clark Kent is Superman,' you repeat to yourself in glee. As you plot what you can do with this information, you also puzzle about the two statements. In 'Clark Kent is Clark Kent' and 'Clark Kent is Superman', both Kent and Superman have the same reference (the son of Jor-El, the Kryptonian). But even though this is true, 'Clark Kent is Superman' is informative in a way the other statement is not.

This gave rise to Frege's key contention. Frege says what this shows is that a word can have the same reference but a difference sense. So 'Superman' and 'Clark Kent' both have the same reference but different senses. In what follows, Frege suggests that the senses which differ between two words are accounted for by their 'mode of presentation'. This would be especially true in the case of Superman and Kent, whose appearance is intended to be deceptively dissimilar.

Important Principles of Language

Compositionality

Compositionality is an intriguing claim that the meaning of a complex expression is entirely dependent on the meaning of its simpler parts along with the arrangement of those parts. The controversy over this view of language is about whether there are exceptions, and more pointedly, whether construing expressions purely on a compositional analysis is adequate for understanding the meaning of those expressions. Critics would point out that compositionality seems to avoid the nuances involved when something is uttered, as well as the intention of the speaker. Allusions and subtleties such as sarcasm and irony would seem to be left out too on this understanding of language.

The general argument in favour of compositionality is that every day we encounter many new sentences to which we have never been exposed. Yet even though we have never seen or heard these complex expressions before, we understand them. On the compositional analysis, we are able to understand because everything we need to know is already there in the sentences (presuming we are a native speaker and have knowledge of both the individual words and the syntactical rules governing the language). Because of this ability, the compositionalists argue that the meaning of the complex statements rests entirely on what can be found in the sentences themselves and nothing outside.

Extension

Extension is a very handy term and concept. Remember that the reference of a word is the reality to which it refers. The reference of 'London' is the actual capital city in England alongside the Thames. 'Extension' is an expansion of the concept of reference. So the extension of 'London', just like its reference, is the capital city in England alongside the Thames. However, extension can apply to more than one object, and words other than nouns can have extension. For instance, 'elephant' has an extension of the class of all elephants, as does the more generic term 'flower' for the class of flowers. But non-nouns, as I mentioned, also have extension. For the verb 'flies', this term has the extension of things which fly: birds, bats, planes etc.

It is important to note that the extension of a word is not the same as the meaning.

London and the River Thames.

A meaning has a more specific application than an extension. The meaning of a word in the context of philosophy of language has often been associated with its 'intension' (the internal content of a concept).

Semantics

How many times have you have heard a variation of the statement 'Now we're just arguing semantics'? The idea is that semantics is something like quibbling over words. That is not quite right. Semantics concerns the meaning of words, what they signify, and so it is central to how any language is understood. One could almost say that semantics are the plain meaning of words when we use them – what a robot might understand if it were capable of understanding you.

Semantics concerns the symbols that people use to represent language, in two senses: both the symbols that language actually uses and, in a more theoretical sense, the way in which any language could make use of symbols, that is, the conditions for how even imagined languages could do so.

The field of semantics should be contrasted with pragmatics. Semantics and pragmatics come from the Greek words for 'sign' and 'action' respectively. So while semantics concerns what words signify, pragmatics deals with all the non-literal elements of an expression which are intended and implied.

Use and Mention

The distinction between use and mention is one which we all recognize, but seldom does it rise to the level of consciousness. By the time we have acquired language, and this is very early in contemporary society, in most circumstances we do not even distinguish between words and the things they refer to. We are even less aware of the distinction between use and mention, because it is even more subtle.

To put it simply, to 'use' a word is the way we customarily make use of words in language. If I say 'I saw a bird', then I am 'using' the word 'bird'. In using it, I am using the word only in so far as it signifies or references the flying animal with two feathered wings. Now consider if I say 'I saw a "bird"'. In this second situation, I was looking at a crossword puzzle my friend had solved. She wrote in the word 'b-i-r-d' as the solution to one of the clues. In this instance I am 'mentioning' the word, because I refer to the word itself, not the animal it refers to.

I have used quotation marks in the second example because, after all, this is a written book. However, the distinction between use and mention is all the more important in spoken speech, when quotation marks are seldom used, though we imagine them in place whenever an instance of mentioning occurs.

THE USE AND MENTION DISTINCTION

USE:
I SEE A BIRD

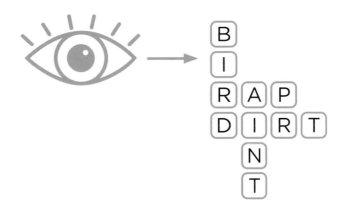

MENTION:
I SEE A 'BIRD'

The use/mention distinction can be quite helpful in a situation in which someone is relating the words of someone else, where those words, on their face value, are offensive or otherwise inadvisable to be uttered on their own. It becomes much more understandable, however, if the person relating the words intends to 'mention' them, and is not 'using' them.

Implicature

The concept of implicature, despite coming across as philosophical jargon, refers to something we do nearly every day. Consider if someone asks 'What should I wear today?' and the answer comes back 'It is chilly outside'. The literal meaning of the sentence only concerns the weather, but the implicature is that since it is chilly outside, *you should wear warm clothing*. Take, in a similar context, 'You should bring your umbrella'. At face value, there is no explicit reason why this means anything other than taking an umbrella, but we know that the implicature of this sentence is something like 'I know it is likely to rain, and I do not want you to get wet. Please take an umbrella with you to prevent this'.

The phrase 'you should bring your umbrella' has the implicature it is raining outside.

The idea of implicature acknowledges that in our conversations a great many things can be implied, and the meaning of the implication depends on the social context in which it occurs. Paul Grice, the philosopher who, in the 1980s, first drew attention to implicature as part of our linguistic practice, thought there were many different rules or maxims which govern its use. The most important of these is the cooperative principle, which posits that conversations take place with a certain goal in mind, and that contributions to the conversation have to stay aligned with this accepted purpose.

There are a number of other maxims which implicitly guide discussions. One must say what one thinks is true, and not what is false. Another is to give the right amount of information, neither too much nor too little, and what is said must be adequately and appropriately informative. Related to this, ambiguity has to be avoided, and contributions have to be brief. There are other maxims as well, each of which exerts an invisible but recognized role in the give and take of human conversation. One reason Grice undertook an inventory of these different types of conversational maxims, which we all seem to obey, is that they help to give an explanation as to how implicature comes about. Since 'it is chilly today' does not, for example, say anything about wearing a wool coat or a bikini, Grice's proposal is that there are underlying rules governing how and when to use the language we do, and that understanding these rules will give us guidance on how implicature comes about.

Vagueness

One of the more captivating puzzles from antiquity concerns the sorites. Sorites was the Greek word for a heap, and the puzzling aspect comes about when determining what constitutes a heap. A single grain is added to another until at some point this becomes a 'heap'. Likewise, when, one by one, grains are removed, at some point we say there is no longer a heap. But how can a single grain of sand determine that something is a heap? And could it really be true that, say, 778 grains (or whatever number we settle upon) constitutes a heap, but 777 does not?

This paradox of the sorites can apply to other terms as well, such as the term 'bald' or 'tall'. Thus a word such as 'heap' or 'bald' seems to be concerned with vagueness, and this involves both our knowledge and what the term itself refers to.

THE SORITES PARADOX

AT WHAT POINT DO WE HAVE A HEAP?

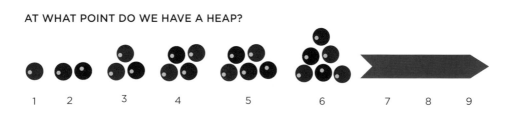

Whatever the solution to the sorites puzzle, it will have to take into account borderline cases and how to explain them. In other words, it will have to show us why there is a border between calling this grouping of sand a heap, while denying a smaller grouping of sand the same description. Some have taken the position that such words as 'bald' are vague descriptions of a set of precise things. Thus the uncertainty of the term would be due to the term itself, but at the same time baldness and the correct designation of 'bald' would seem to be assessed numerically since, presented with a man, one has to evaluate whether he is bald or not (with a strict divide between the bald and not bald). However, others press forward the idea that it is this very ambiguity which shows us that the term baldness cannot refer to a precise number of hairs or heads on which those hairs are found. There are some cases, in other words, where it is neither true nor false that a head is bald. We simply are not in a position to call it true or false.

Speech Act Theory

Ancient Greek thinkers, historians, poets and philosophers alike all extolled the pursuit of virtue 'in words and in deeds'. Speech act theory is a 20th-century theory putting forward the idea that speech itself is a kind of action. If that idea seems far-fetched, here are two examples to make it more palpable. A minister overseeing a wedding marries a couple by the very fact of saying 'I now declare you man and wife'. A member of the royal family christens a boat by smashing a champagne bottle on the bow and conferring a name upon the boat.

A speech act has three main parts, as first put forth by the philosopher J.L. Austin. The most obvious of these is the locutionary act. This consists of the sounds uttered by a speaker. They must follow the conventional rules, syntax and grammar of the language under consideration. One cannot say, for instance, 'Polka dot spot fridging purplelessly upon the impossible leaves'. At least one cannot say this and have it fall under a locutionary act in speech act theory.

There is also the illocutionary act: the intention a speaker has in producing the locutionary act. For instance, imagine someone comes up to the hostess at a restaurant and asks 'Do you have a table for two?'. Taken on its face value, the hostess would not be wrong if she simply replied 'Yes', for the restaurant does in fact have a table with only two seats. As it turns out, however, the table is occupied. We know, as part of the linguistic community in which 'Do you have a table for two?' is uttered, that the intent of the question is not to determine the physical layout out of the restaurant. The real question is to ask whether or not the restaurant has a suitable table for two, and if it is unoccupied, could it be given to the occupier. This is the illocutionary force of what has been said.

There is one more element, the perlocutionary act. This act is the actual effect the utterance someone has made has on the audience. In the case above, the perloctionary force of the question would be the restaurant hostess saying no or yes, taking down the name of the person, or whatever other response she would have to the question.

SPEECH ACT THEORY

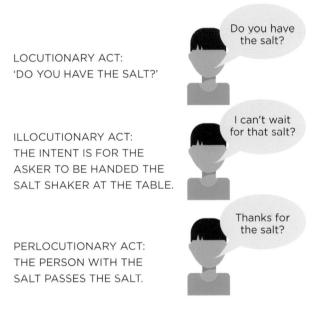

LOCUTIONARY ACT:
'DO YOU HAVE THE SALT?'

Do you have the salt?

ILLOCUTIONARY ACT:
THE INTENT IS FOR THE
ASKER TO BE HANDED THE
SALT SHAKER AT THE TABLE.

I can't wait for that salt?

PERLOCUTIONARY ACT:
THE PERSON WITH THE
SALT PASSES THE SALT.

Thanks for the salt?

Types and Tokens

The distinction between types and tokens is a useful linguistic method of classification. It is somewhat similar to the old logical and linguistic disputes in the Middle Ages centring around what universals and particulars are.

Suppose you and a friend visit a public park together for the first time. When you return, a third friend asks both of you how many trees were there. You say ten and your friend says three. You voice your disagreement at this number, and ask why your friend said three. She says, 'I counted three oaks, three pines and four elm trees.' This friend counted the types of tree: there were three kinds of trees. On the other hand you counted by token, and there were ten individual trees.

When it comes to language use, there appears to be a strong human inclination to recognize the distinction between token and type. The linguistic distinction tallies with a psychological distinction whereby we categorize things as belonging to a class or kind of thing. Whatever the ultimate explanation for this parallel development of logic and language, it suggests that prior to evaluations of value, or comparison, or more subtle distinctions, the basic separation between type and token is a feature of our daily thought process.

TYPE AND TOKEN

2 *TYPES* OF TREE: PALM, PINE

5 *TOKENS*: 3 PALM, 2 PINE.

Universal Grammar

The theory of universal grammar, formulated by Noam Chomsky (b. 1928), aims to solve a developmental problem central to the psychology of language. This puzzle, dubbed 'Plato's problem' by Chomsky, asks how it is that language progresses from a very modest beginning in early childhood to the sophisticated state it achieves in adulthood. On Chomsky's reckoning, saying that language is entirely innate is to concede the development of language to nature, whereas to say that newborns are nothing more than a blank slate is to concede that language acquisition owes entirely to nurture.

Between the extremes of nature and nurture, Chomsky suggested a middle course whereby we are equipped from birth with a certain kind of structure, and through experience and age we build upon this structure until we have reached mature competence. This structure was called by Chomsky 'universal grammar', because it is shared as a feature

Noam Chomsky.

Language is a game, governed by rules, with the words making up the pieces on the board, with some actions allowed and others forbidden.

of all languages, not only as a matter of historical fact but of linguistic possibility. This universal grammar sets the parameters for later language use, like a primordial substrate, whether the language is Latin, Swahili, Akkadian or English.

Private Language

An interesting contrast to universal grammar, although it is a complementary concept, is the idea of a private language – a language which is understood by just one person and would be unlearnable for anyone other than its lone speaker. However, an argument famously advocated by Ludwig Wittgenstein makes the case that possessing a private language is actually impossible. The reasoning is that all languages make use of certain rules in order to confer meanings, and that these rules of language are shaped by the rules of a given speaking community of a language. This means it is simply impossible for there to be a private language, on Wittgenstein's analysis, since an individual by themselves is incapable of performing this role of the community.

Language Games

The objection that Wittgenstein lodges against private language clearly depends on a robust role for rules in language. This can be taken even farther, and Wittgenstein analogized language to a game. Understanding language as a language *game* plays up two aspects in particular. The first is that language is a social activity, with roles to be played by speaker and listener. The second element is that the knowledge of words by itself does not grant someone the ability to speak in a language. What is needed is a knowledge of the rules governing the proper use of words in the context of the language. It is this latter fact which makes language, by analogy, a game. In a game it is never enough to simply know the pieces on the board, which are equivalent to the words in a language, but one must also know the rules of the game. Such rules exist in language no less than in a game. Just as in a game, in language some moves are more or less appropriate to the goal under consideration, while some actions are not allowed at all.

The Sapir-Whorf hypothesis argues that the language we speak determines our thoughts.

Linguistic Relativity/Linguistic Determinism

This concept, also known as the Sapir-Whorf hypothesis, gained prominence from the 1930s. Stated in its strongest form, the idea is that the language we possess dictates the ideas we possess. If you are an English speaker reading this sentence, for example, and only speak English, then English determines the thoughts that you have. The claim can also be modified to state that at the very least the language someone possesses influences their thought, and perhaps even with significant differences between different languages. Evidence for this weaker version of the hypothesis could be the historical fact that philosophical schools tended to be in one area and share a common language, or the observation that different expressions of a world religion like Christianity tend to differ significantly where the language differs.

One fascinating example of the hypothesis is the link between mathematical words and arithmetic. The Hottentot language has words for 'one', 'two' and, in excess of these terms, 'many', but lacks words for any larger units. Speakers of this language are unable to

LINGUISTIC DETERMINISM

WORDS ARE A CAGE, AND ONLY IN THEM CAN OUR THOUGHTS LIVE, OR A PAIR OF SPECTACLES, AND ONLY THROUGH THEM CAN WE SEE.

to conduct even basic mathematical operations, and proponents of linguistic relativism would say this is only because their language does not possess the words to allow them to think mathematically.

The Principles of Language and You

We have surveyed a number of different philosophers and philosophical principles in this chapter. Some of the ideas are disputed, such as the Sapir-Whorf hypothesis, while others, such as the distinction between the signification of words and what they reference, seem indisputable. The central message of the philosophy of language is clear: in order to think well, you have to be able to use words well. Put another way, the more you know of words and about words, the more you know. Whether it is knowing the fallacious arguments that can be employed or just knowing different analyses which can be applied to words, thinking about words is as important as thinking with words. When we are clear about what words do and what they cannot do, we are in a much better position to speak and think clearly, correctly and with precision.

SUMMARY POINTS

- Plato saw that there is a difference between words and the realities which they signify.
- Francis Bacon thought that language arose amid the common hubbub of everyday life and so was ill-equipped for technical use in philosophy and science.
- Thomas Hobbes said that only through language can we grasp the concept of a universal.
- René Descartes centred human rationality on the ability to use language.
- Gottfried Leibniz viewed words as approximations, not perfect representations.
- For Gottlob Frege, language is a carrier of thought, a shell under which lies the important meat of concepts and ideas.
- Speech act theory posits that speech can work much the way that actions do.
- Wittgenstein compared the way we use language to a game, in that it has necessary social aspects like a game and has rules that have to be followed.
- The central idea of linguistic determinism is that the words we use shape the way we think.

The philosophy of mind is at once complex and commonplace.

THE PRINCIPLES OF MIND

The philosophy of mind is at once complex and commonplace. It has to do with the way that the mind, in particular the human mind, works. It may come as a surprise, but to even distinguish the mind as a special entity of its own involves some philosophical reasoning. The history of the mind as an object of philosophy goes back a very long way. Philosophy of mind not only examines the sophisticated psychology of the human mind, but also the nature of thought, both how thoughts are used and how they should be used.

Questions

What is a mind? Do I have a mind? Do animals or plants have minds? Is the mind the same thing as intelligence, or consciousness, or soul or something else? What is the relationship between the mind and the body? Can the mind be reduced to something merely physical, the brain? Are the mind and body two fundamentally different types of substances, and if so how is it that they are able to interact and influence each other, especially in the unity of a human person?

History of Philosophy of Mind

The history of philosophy of mind is tied up with the concept of the soul. Since both concepts are difficult to comprehend, defining one in terms of the other is perhaps not very helpful. But this association of soul and mind began to be made as early as Homer in the eighth century BCE, and by several centuries later Plato was explicitly correlating the form of life, immortal in his view, with the intellectual part of the mind. The philosophy of mind overlaps to a great degree with what we call psychology, and this should be no surprise, for *psyche* was the ancient Greek word for soul, and it is with the soul as mind that we come to think of psychology as the science of the mind.

It can probably be said that as soon as humans discern a difference between two things, there is a pull to make the two entirely separate. This has certainly been the case

The Greek Goddess Psyche, whose name was also the word for soul.

when it comes to the distinction between the mind and body. One of the chief concerns of the philosophy of mind has been to explain the relationship between the two.

Plato discusses the relationship between the body and soul in several of his dialogues. According to the Platonic view, the soul is something invisible, immaterial, and above all divine and immortal. As you may have guessed, the soul is defined largely by contrast to the body. The body is material, visible and subject to change.

By this schema, the soul has a tripartite division into logical, spirited and appetitive parts. The logical part of the soul contains rationality, while the spirited part is responsible for our competitive spirit, loving honour and spirited emotions like anger. In a well-ordered soul the logical and spirited part work in unison, with the spirited subordinate to the logical, to accomplish good for the whole human person. These two parts work together to subdue the malign influence of the appetitive part of the soul. It is this part of the soul that accounts for our bodily desires for sex and food.

PLATO'S TRIPARTITE DIVISION OF THE SOUL: LOGICAL, SPIRITED, APPETITIVE

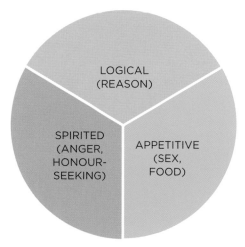

Plato's evidence for these distinctions between various parts of the soul was that at different times we have different factions desiring different things within us. He thought that this was strong evidence for a division of the soul, because he could not see how it could be possible for the same soul to desire two different things at the same time. For instance, how could I want to eat a piece of chocolate while at the same time not want to eat it? By Plato's thinking, there have to be two different factions, or parts, within the soul, each aiming for a different goal. In the example above, the logical part of the soul wishes to moderate chocolate intake for the benefit of health, while the appetitive part of the soul seeks to satiate brute hunger or desire for a pleasurable taste.

Aristotle's *De Anima*

Aristotle's view of the soul and mind was highly influenced by Plato. Once again, what we see in Aristotle is that the mind is fundamentally connected to the soul. The Latin name for Aristotle's treatise on the soul, *De Anima*, is a translation of the Greek *Peri Psyches*. Aristotle also made a three-fold division of soul, though it differs from Plato's, consisting of nutritive, perceptual and rational (or logical) parts. Aristotle was very much concerned with the question of what the soul is in a general sense, and for him plants as

ARISTOTLE'S DIVISION OF SOUL

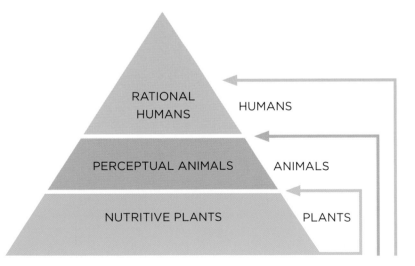

well as animals possess souls. So the nutritive part of the soul is shared by plant, animal and human, and it is this part that is responsible for the growth and maintenance of the whole organism. The perceptual part of the soul is responsible for sense perception, as well as all the cognitive processes associated with it, such as memory and experience. Both animals and humans possess the perceptual part of the soul. The part of the soul belonging to humans alone is the rational part.

In Aristotle's psychology there is a necessary relationship between body and soul. This is his famous idea of hylomorphism, which simply means that the human organism is an association of matter (Greek *hyle*) and form (Greek *morphe*). Aristotle tells us that the form of a body is its soul; the doctrine of hylomorphism is in a literal sense a 'body-soulism'.

Stoic and Epicurean Views of the Soul

The Stoics and Epicureans offer an interesting view of the soul, because they were both committed to the idea that everything which exists is matter. The Stoics believed that the soul was a mixture of fire and air. These were the two lightest elements, and since warm air is a feature of our breathing, they reasoned that this owed to a mixture of those two elements. The body, on the other hand, was composed of water and earth. The Stoics believed that the soul was entirely rational and was a single, partless mind.

The soul was also material in the philosophy of the Epicureans. However, they believed that it was made of very fine and round atoms, the finest that exist. The Epicureans held that in order to produce thinking, the fastest of all actions, the soul atoms have to be able move very quickly – they have to be fine enough to move throughout the body to make an arm move with immediacy as soon as the thought is produced.

René Descartes

Moving on to the 17th century, the view of René Descartes on the makeup of the soul is as simple as it has been influential. It is often termed Cartesian dualism, for as much as any other philosopher before him, Descartes says that there are two substances, body and soul. Body is known as that which is spatially extended, while soul or mind is that which is a thinking thing. The mind is not extended into space but is defined and determined by the mental states it possesses: feeling, doubting, believing, knowing, perceiving, reasoning and so forth.

This view of the mind is controversial, for it seems to irreconcilably split mind and body apart from each other in such a way that it is hard to imagine how the mind could influence, much less cause anything to happen in, the human body, and vice versa.

CARTESIAN DUALISM	
SOUL	**BODY**
THINKING	EXTENDED
FEELING	HARD
DOUBTING	SOFT
BELIEVING	HOT
KNOWING	COLD
PERCEIVING	COLOURED
REASONING	WET
	DRY

Nicolas Malebranche

The philosophical position of Malebranche, who followed on the heels of Descartes, is a direct response to the difficulty posed by Cartesian dualism. Malebranche considered that in Cartesianism, body and mind are causally incompatible, and proposed resolving this through the idea that any apparent interaction between the two is merely an 'occasion' on which God intervenes, in order, for instance, to make the mind feel the pain of a bee sting on the body, or for the hand to hold an apple when it is told to do so by the mind.

Nicolas Malebranche.

George Berkeley and Idealism

Berkeley (1685–1753) is responsible for one of the most imaginative and at the same time one of the most unintuitive positions in the history of philosophy, idealism. He believed that everything in the world was either mind or dependent on mind.

The result was a very elaborate system, which, while it has gained many detractors, has turned out very difficult to disprove. For concision we will look at only two of Berkeley's reasons for holding to idealism.

First, it is important to keep in mind that Berkeley actually denied that there are material substances: everything that exists is related directly to and dependent on a mind (although that can include the mind of God). His famous dictum encapsulating his philosophy was 'Esse est percipi', 'To exist is to be perceived'.

All of human knowledge, according to Berkeley, comes about in one of three ways: perception, introspection or reflection, or

George Berkeley.

imagination. Yet all of these are ideas of a kind. Even something extremely palpable, such as eating an apple, is experienced only as an idea. The touch of the apple's hard skin, the red gleaming colour and the taste of the crisp apple are only ideas operating in your mind. You confuse the apple being an idea in your mind with it being a real material thing.

Berkeley's 'master argument' was meant to be the final blow to someone's belief that what they see out in the world are actually material objects. Consider, he says, whatever you want – apples, animals, cookies, planets, fairy tales, emotions – all of these are nothing but ideas. We can know this because, as soon as we consider them, we see that this idea of an apple, for example, corresponds directly with our experience of an apple. What we think an apple is matches the experience we have gained from apples. Both are ideas of apples. So we cannot help but think of everything in terms of ideas, because everything

BERKELEY'S MASTER ARGUMENT

EVEN AN ENCOUNTER WITH SOMETHING AS 'SOLID' AS AN
APPLE IS AN EXPERIENCE OF AN IDEA OF AN APPLE.

ultimately is an idea.

Immanuel Kant

Kant's view of the workings of the mind gives insight into his whole philosophical project. Central to his work was the concept of *a priori* knowledge. This is knowledge which is acquired independently of experience, not derived from it. Kant said that the mind possesses some knowledge that is *a priori*: it has not been learned or taught, nor can it be. Our possession of this knowledge is itself an *a priori* truth – it cannot be discovered through experience, but our minds must be assumed to have been constructed in this way in order to make progress in the philosophy of mind. What are the *a priori* concepts which Kant is referring to? They are quantity: unity, plurality and totality; quality: reality, negation and limitation; relation: inherence and subsistence, causality and dependence, and community; modality: possibility and impossibility, existence and non-existence, necessity and contingency.

Kant's philosophical method is consistent. The point about how the mind possessing these *a priori* truths is itself an *a priori* truth now comes into play as a factor. Kant is not only saying that this is the way your or my mind works; he is making the claim that any kind of mind must work as he is describing. This works itself out in another important way in Kant's philosophy. According to him we have to make assumptions about the way experience is possible, for only by determining what makes experience possible will we arrive at the necessary conditions for rational minds to exist in the first place. It is not conceivable, on this approach, to think of a rational mind without the concepts of causality or unity for example. Kant calls this the transcendental deduction. It is transcendental in the sense that it goes beyond all empirical experience.

Kant's own theorizing about consciousness is best understood in light of this transcendental deduction. He thinks the 'we' or 'I' or self-consciousness is to be identified as the knowledge one has of one's own experience.

A PRIORI CONCEPTS OF THE MIND

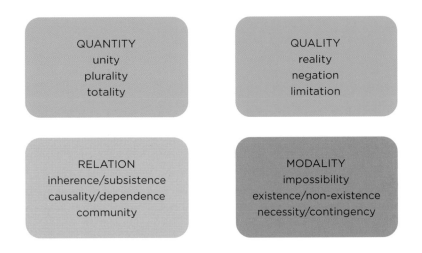

QUANTITY
unity
plurality
totality

QUALITY
reality
negation
limitation

RELATION
inherence/subsistence
causality/dependence
community

MODALITY
impossibility
existence/non-existence
necessity/contingency

Franz Brentano

Brentano (1838–1917) is a seminal figure for the field of psychology and different areas of philosophy of mind. Some of the more important contributions he made are in the realm of consciousness and intentionality.

We all would probably admit that we have an understanding of what consciousness is, even if we cannot define it. A mental state is something we seem to possess by virtue of being alive and awake, whether it is an active awareness of a bee buzzing or a preoccupation with an awkward social encounter earlier in the day.

Brentano offers up a number of fascinating insights into the nature of consciousness. Consider, for example, the analysis he gives of how presentation works in the human mind. You are watching a horse gallop across a field. One could say there are two things happening: the presentation (how the horse appears) of the horse as it is in the world and the presentation of the horse as it appears in the mind. But as we experience our perception of the horse, the presentation of it in our mind and our grasping of the presentation are perceived as one and the same thing. To put it Brentano's way, the mind

Franz Brentano.

When seeing this scene, you see both the horse galloping and yourself seeing the horse.

directs itself toward something in a primary sense, but is also aware of itself doing so in an incidental or secondary sense. So when I look at the horse I see the horse primarily, but I also see myself seeing the horse. There are two objects I see: the horse as a presentation to my mind, and the presentation to myself of this presentation. One can appreciate how this recursive explanation of the way perception works as a good provisional insight into the definition of consciousness.

Since Brentano believed that all mental activity shares this feature of possessing a primary object while the mind itself is the secondary object, this means that he denied that there could be anything resembling an unconscious act. As part of this commitment, Brentano also said consciousness always forms a unity. This can be understood as saying that any time we have a mental object in mind, whether perceiving a car or wondering where a long-lost lover now lives, we can only have in mind that single object, our minds cannot 'multi-task', at least not simultaneously in any single instant. An analogy that gets this idea across is that although you can have many different apps on your phone open at the same time, your screen will only display at any given time one of the programs. The screen is analogous to consciousness while the different apps are different mental objects.

BRENTANO'S UNITY OF CONSCIOUSNESS

 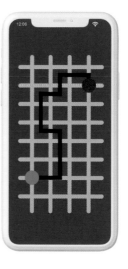

THE MIND IS LIKE A SMARTPHONE – IT CAN ONLY DISPLAY AND
EXPERIENCE ONE 'PROGRAM' AT A TIME.

Epiphenomenalism

By the late 19th century the balance of thinking had shifted, and was giving more weight to body than to mind. Epiphenomenalism reduces the power of the mind to such a degree that it turns it into a mere side effect. The theory is that thoughts, and all cognitive events for that matter, have only physical causes (and cannot themselves cause physical effects). The internal workings of the body, from a biological and physiological vantage point, are nothing more than the end result of a long chain of causes. It is not so much that one thought doesn't cause another but that physiological processes are responsible for both at a higher level of remove.

Emergentism

This is a theory of the mind not too far removed from epiphenomenalism. Whereas epiphenomenalism focuses on the disjunction between thought and body by declaring that thought is a product of the body, emergentism, on the other hand, looks at this same relationship and says that consciousness and thought emerge, inexplicably, from the natural arrangement of the body and brain. This grants to the mind the kind of mysterious and apparently irreducible properties it seems to possess.

Important Principles of Mind

Subjectivity and Personal Identity

Questions revolving around who we are have played a central role in philosophical thought for ages. But the assumption behind these inquiries is that we are a person, we have an identity that persists over time and fundamentally there is a real 'me' that can be identified.

Part of the justification for our belief in a 'true self' at the centre of our personality is the special access we have to our thoughts. This front-row seat to our own thoughts has several unique features. One is that we, by having thoughts, have immediate access to them. This means both that thoughts are accessible to us the moment we have them and that they are not mediated through some other means. Our thoughts grant direct access to themselves. A practical outcome of this fact is that what we say we are thinking is in fact what we are thinking. Another person cannot come along and say 'You are not really thinking that or believing that or tasting that'.

The subjective experience we have in consciousness also has another distinct feature:

it is a united perspective. This is not a claim about the objects we are paying attention to, but rather the idea that everything seems to be funnelled or directed to a single position, the focal point of our thoughts, which we associate with our consciousness. Furthermore, this perspective cannot be shared or accessed by anything or anyone else. The perspective we hold as our consciousness is a window which no one else can see out of it. It's as if we live in a house with a one-way mirror and no doors. We can see everything outside of the house, but since there are no doors and this is the only window, we cannot experience the outside world except through this window of consciousness. Because the window is a one-way mirror on the outside, no one else, in turn, can see into the private realm we deem our conscious self.

CONSCIOUSNESS AS AN INESCAPABLE HOUSE

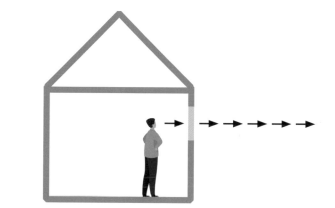

A HOUSE WITH NO DOORS AND A SINGLE WINDOW,
WITH A ONE-WAY MIRROR TO THE OUTSIDE.

Consciousness as an Inner Monitor

A slightly different construal of consciousness is that it is not a co-awareness which attends every thought, such as advocated by Franz Brentano, but a special internal awareness which is usually but not always active. On this basis, consciousness is something that occasionally wavers. Imagine you are doing something repetitive and perhaps even monotonous, like mowing the lawn or driving long-distance. Advocates of the internal awareness view of consciousness would point to occasional lapses of awareness, instances where our consciousness pulls back, while other operations of the mind still take place in the foreground, as evidence that what we call consciousness is actually a process to monitor our other internal processes.

Qualia

Qualia as a term is a plural noun derived from the Latin word from which we get the English 'quality'. We would do well, in fact, to understand qualia to be the qualities of the mental states we experience. To put it another way, there is a certain subjective experience you undergo when you eat a strawberry ice cream or you scratch your knee or you kiss your first love. These states of mind seem to share certain features. One is that it is hard to imagine how these private mental states can be explained wholly by appealing to the processes of the brain. At least by one construal of qualia, they provide evidence that the mind cannot be reduced to the brain. The idea here is that even knowing everything about how the brain works would never be enough to grant us the insider experience such as mental states evidently provide us. Qualia, viewed together as a feature of the mind, are taken to be a central element of consciousness.

A strawberry ice-cream cone provides a particular subjective experience.

Mental Phenomena

We might take for granted that there are distinct things we call 'mental phenomena'. But how do we distinguish between mental and non-mental phenomena? We are so used to thinking with thoughts that we seldom take time to think about our thoughts!

One position is that mental phenomena are distinguished by the privacy that a thinker has in having them. If I alone know where the secret treasure is buried, then someone cannot peer into my mind to take that information out. Thought is uniquely privileged and limited to the thinking subject.

There is a sense, even if it must be moderated to an extent, that our experience of our thoughts is infallible in a way that our thoughts of other things or of other people are not. For instance, it cannot be false that I am currently feeling cheerful, if in fact I feel cheerful.

Panpsychism

This theory strikes some as strange and some as obvious. 'Panpsychism' (from the Greek *pan* and *psyche*) means 'all-soul-ism'. It is the view that the entire universe has mental properties of one kind or another. In this sense, everything is soul. A large part of the motivation for panpsychism is the apparent uniqueness of mental phenomena when contrasted with the bodily. There are such things as thought, consciousness, qualia and so forth, and brute matter cannot account for all of these mental properties. On the panpsychic view, mind has equal footing with corporeal matter as a fundamental unit of the universe.

Similarly, it does not seem reasonable to the panpsychist to say that the mind can *emerge* from matter. If it is true that bones and sinews and flesh, for example, do not by themselves possess mental qualities, then it must be the case that the combination of these different physical elements accounts for mental qualities. Yet this does not appear defensible as a proposition either, so the panpsychist instead adopts the position that everything has some mental properties, including bones, sinews and flesh. The end result is to conclude that everything in the universe, including the fundamental units of matter, possesses 'soul'.

Perception

Throughout this chapter we have discussed various conceptions of and issues concerning consciousness. Closely related to consciousness is the idea of perception, chiefly the input we receive from our five sense organs, though usually the focus is given to the sense of sight.

Perception can thus be understood as the mental process which humans make use of through physical means to understand and interpret the world outside the body. Perception in some sense seems to be prior to or more fundamental than consciousness, because perception is what is given to consciousness to be made sense of.

Aristotle made a helpful distinction between imagination and perception which helps to bring out the uniqueness of perception. He said that we can imagine something at any time, whether it is in front of us or not. However, in the case of perception, provided the sense organs are working correctly, when an object of perception is presented, for example, to the eyes, we cannot help but see the bed or car or whatever it is set before us. So perception has objects, and the object must be present to the sense organ in order to be perceived.

Intentionality

Another way to distinguish the mental from the non-mental is to appeal to 'intentionality'. This is a concept, revivified by Franz Brentano from medieval logic, that there is a subject and object for every thought. The subject is whoever happens to be having the thought, while the object is that which is thought about. This object doesn't have to be a physical object, it could be an abstract idea such as justice, or it could even be a thought about something that doesn't exist, like Santa Claus.

Although there is a huge variety of mental phenomena, from hatred to judgement to a visual presentation, what all of these have in common is that they are *about* something. There is a hatred *of* sushi, a judgement *that* the maths equation is correct, a visual presentation *of* a painting. In a manner of speaking these are objects internal to the thoughts that have them. In ordinary language we would say they are *in* the mind.

A mosaic of the god Poseidon.

At any rate, it is clear that when we have a thought, there is something the thought is about. We call this the intentional object of our thought. It is easier to understand the concept of an intentional object if you think of a non-existent object. Think of Poseidon, god of water. Even though he does not exist, he is present in your mind as an intentional object, as something which your thought concerns or is directed towards, whatever that thought may be.

Logical Behaviourism

In the 20th century Carl Hempel introduced a novel way of formulating psychological states, in terms of behaviour or otherwise observable states. This idea stemmed from a larger commitment to the philosophy of logical positivism, a system which maintains that truth needs to be verified empirically. In particular logical behaviourism says that psychological states can be translated into the arena of the physical and observable.

To be clear, this is not, properly speaking, something concerning only the philosophy of mind. It is a theory which uses philosophy of mind as a means to discuss how we can speak about other minds. If the psychological state of someone cannot be reformulated into physical and behavioural terms, then the psychological statement should not be considered true. The peculiarity of this system is that it assumes that for all psychological states there are observable and consistent behaviours that attend that state. This is probably more true in the case of someone mourning a loved one, for example, and less true in the case of someone experiencing their first taste of a new food.

Free Will

No philosophical discussion is as intriguing or has as many important repercussions as the issue of free will. The 18th-century man of letters Samuel Johnson said that all experience is for, and all theory against, the idea of free will. Free will, of course, does reflect our instinctive view of the mind and how it works.

Free will is a difficult issue to grapple with and even to define. In the broadest sense it means to be unconstrained by outside factors when making decisions. Control over one's own decisions or actions is at the heart of free will.

One central issue of free will is its relationship to determinism. Determinism is the idea that the current state of the world at a given moment necessitates one and only one state of affairs in the future. Pretend that everything in the world is arranged in the same way on multiple occasions, then what happens after each of those occasions would be exactly the same each time. This is determinism.

Samuel Johnson.

The question then arises whether free will is compatible with determinism. The view that there can be both free will and determinism at the same time is called compatibilism. One argument against this position is the idea that having free will means what we do is up to us. If we have the freedom to do or not do a given action, then we are free. But the events of history along with the laws of nature are not up to us – we did not decide what came before us. The argument then is that, since we are not responsible for the events and circumstances which came before us, we are not responsible for the effects which they caused. On the assumption of determinism, these pre-existing conditions would be responsible for all the choices and actions I undertake.

Multiple Realizability

DETERMINISM

THE ARRANGEMENT OF MOVING SHAPES
AT TIME A WILL DETERMINE THE ARRANGEMENT AT TIME B

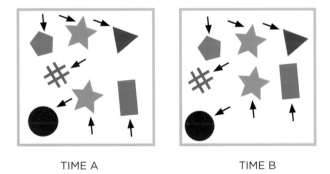

TIME A   TIME B

With the expansion of scientific knowledge of the brain, especially in neuroscience and cognitive science, many philosophers have become convinced that the mind is nothing more than the brain. The mind is to be identified as the brain. At a more minute level, this entails that all states of the mind are states of the brain. But Hilary Putnam, working in the later 20th century, offered an objection to this thesis. If we take for granted that states of the mind are interchangeable with states of matter, he argued, then this would suggest, for example, that our experience of pain owes to the configuration of our brain. Yet there are many different animals with different brain structures from our own which

Hilary Putnam.

seem to experience pain as well. So if the mind–brain identity theory is correct, why is it that seemingly different brain arrangements can result in the same kind of mind states? Furthermore, he pursued the logical consequence of mind–brain identification, asking whether pain can be realized in different types of biological bodies. Imagine we encounter an alien life form with a completely different physical makeup. His contemporary Jerry Fodor then makes the point that we wouldn't assume these aliens were incapable of pain simply because they have a different biological makeup. Thus the multiple realization objection says that pain, or another mental phenomenon, is and can be realized in multiple different life forms, and therefore the mind cannot be correlated directly to the brain.

Anomalous Monism

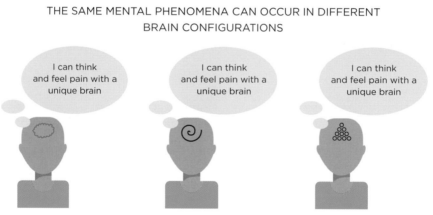

MULTIPLE REALIZABILITY

THE SAME MENTAL PHENOMENA CAN OCCUR IN DIFFERENT
BRAIN CONFIGURATIONS

I can think and feel pain with a unique brain

I can think and feel pain with a unique brain

I can think and feel pain with a unique brain

In direct response to the multiple realization objection, Donald Davidson posited 'anomalous monism', sometimes identified with the less intimidating-sounding 'token-identity theory'. This theory attempts to escape the multiple realization objection by carefully articulating the way in which the makeup of the brain corresponds to different mental states.

Davidson arrived at his theory by observing that mental events can cause physical events, and physical events can cause mental events. When there is this kind of causal influence, the causation is strict and lawlike, there can be no exceptions. In other words, if the physical makeup of the brain is arranged in a certain way, then the mind will necessarily enter into a certain mental state. Yet there was an interesting feature of mental states which Davidson observed, namely that, even though we would expect strict lawlike behaviour for mental events, they do not seem to have a direct correlation to any one physical state of the brain.

In order to make sense of this discrepancy, we need a theory that explains mental events in terms of physical events in the brain while also showing why mental states do not follow a strict law. Davidson's solution was to say all mental events are physical events, but he did so in a way that avoided attributing laws between mental and physical events. To put this as clearly as possible, Davidson meant that if mental event A causes a physical event B, then A must be a physical event as well. Thus he takes it to be the case that every mental event is connected to a physical event at some level of interaction.

Functionalism

This is a theory which defines mental states in terms of the function such states serve in the context of a whole organism or system. The earliest parts of such a system can be seen as early as Aristotle, who defined the human soul as a set of capacities realized for the purpose of living.

In some forms of functionalism, the human being can be analogized to a sophisticated

FUNCTIONALISM

THE MIND IS A COMPLEX MACHINE, RECEIVING INPUTS
AND SENDING OUTPUTS

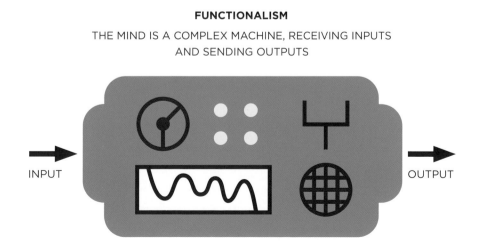

INPUT

OUTPUT

robot which receives various inputs and in return issues outputs, or behaves in a given way. The language becomes technical, but in the functionalist scenario, a person is imagined to be in a certain state, where 'state' means nothing more than being disposed to act a certain way if certain conditions are met. For example, a functionalist would say of a pedestrian waiting at a crossing that if the pedestrian desires to cross the street and the crossing sign turns green as an input, then the output will be walking across the street.

Principles of Mind and You

The depth and breadth of thinking about the mind can be overwhelming, and we have only touched upon some of the main figures and ideas found in it. Although we are so accustomed to thinking, we are also very unfamiliar with thinking about our thinking, in terms of understanding how our thoughts work or are acquired, or what it is that does the thinking, so to speak, on our behalf. Yet delving into a self-analysis is rewarding, for it delivers us a knowledge of the self we will find nowhere else. We study the philosophy of mind chiefly not to find out how the human mind works but because we want to find

The oracle at Delphi.

out how our individual minds do so. The Delphic oracle in ancient Greece was famous for the inscription greeting visitors to the shrine, 'Know Thyself'. It is by investigating the nature of consciousness and the relationship of the mind to the body, as well as other related concepts, that we come to understand ourselves better.

SUMMARY POINTS

- The history of the mind is tied up with the history of the soul, and both have typically been distinguished from the body.
- Plato split the soul into logical, spirited and appetitive parts.
- Aristotle also had a tripartite division of the soul, with logical, perceptual and nutritive parts of the soul.
- The Stoics believed that the soul had no parts, was essentially rational, and was made of fire and air.
- Cartesian dualism offers two radically different substances: body is extended, and mind is a thinking thing.
- George Berkeley argued that everything in the world is either mind or the product of mind.
- Immanuel Kant's proposal of how the mind works presupposes the necessary conditions to make rationality possible.
- Franz Brentano believed that when we have a mental object in mind, there are in a sense two objects: the primary object, such as a setting sun, and the incidental object, our inner mental state as we observe the setting sun.
- Qualia are the subjective elements of experience.
- Intentionality is the acknowledgement that every thought has some 'object' which the thought concerns, whether that's a cloud or an invisible angel.

Chapter 8

THE PRINCIPLES OF AESTHETICS

The roots of aesthetic experience and the philosophical study of beauty, which is one way to characterize the philosophy of aesthetics, go back to ancient Greece. The word 'aesthetic', in fact, is derived from the Greek word for physical perception. But it would be wrong to think that aesthetics is confined to the visual or deals only with perception, void of any thinking or rationality. The perception involved in the field of aesthetics is often rational, reflective and philosophical.

A large part of this chapter will be dealing with two concepts: beauty and art. Sometimes these two terms are very closely aligned, perhaps even equated, but this is not always the case. For instance, we can easily see something beautiful in nature, such as a sunset in the mountains, and we do not consider this art. Often disputes about the meaning of art centre around different conceptions of beauty and the practical understanding of beauty is often to be identified in the framework of art.

Questions

What is beauty? Is beauty something that is only visual? Can aesthetic taste be taught? Is there a moral quality to aesthetics? Are there rules or principles that must be followed for something to appear beautiful? What is art? What is the purpose of art?

History of Philosophy of Aesthetics

If we go back to Plato's time, the Athenian philosopher had more than a few things to say about beauty and art. Although he had an uneven relationship with art, he sometimes praised it directly. For instance in the dialogue *Ion*, Socrates says that poetry comes to poets directly from the gods. Plato, like everyone else in the Athenian society of his time, made no clear distinction between what was beautiful and what was good. This is true in the adjective for 'beautiful' (*kalos*) which can also mean 'noble'; it is also true in the formulation of their word for a 'good and noble man', *kaloskagathos*, which was really three words smashed together into one inseparable concept. Importantly, in Plato and through his influence, beauty makes an ethical claim on us. It is good to pursue beauty and it is natural to pursue what is good.

So Plato afforded beauty a prominent place in his philosophy, even remarking in his dialogue *Phaedrus* that beauty alone among the Forms has the distinct privilege of being visually stunning. But he also is clear that the individual instances of beauty on earth, and more particularly art, are in some sense inferior to the unseen realm of eternal Forms.

It is in the midst of this philosophical commitment that Plato puts forth his idea that art is imitation. The Greek word which Plato used to describe this process, *mimesis*, is still in use today. *Mimesis* means imitation and, in Plato's thinking especially, applies to the imitation or copying of nature. One of the central measures for identifying the success of mimesis is the degree to which the copy is a faithful depiction of the original. However, in Plato's view, even the more accurate representations of art are still fundamentally flawed, because art is an inferior copy of an original Form that is perfect in every way. Even worse, that copy does not directly represent the original, but is several steps removed from it. It is a copy of a copy.

PLATO: ART AS IMITATION

BEAUTIFUL ORIGINAL OF NATURE   INFERIOR COPY OF ART

Aristotelian Aesthetics

Aristotle also weighed in on the importance of beauty and art. In his *Metaphysics* he seems to suggest that beauty is something that comes about through symmetry, size or proportion. The beauty of Aristotle is immanent, and unlike the transcendental beauty of Plato, resides within the individual things which possess it. Nor is beauty unchanging as it is for Plato – the beauty that someone has changes with age and the actions they perform. A youth is beautiful, if indeed he is, for a different reason than an older man is. Beauty is not necessarily visual either. Developing the idea that a thing's beauty is determined by it performing its natural function, in *On the Parts of Animals* Aristotle urges us to appreciate the beauty of all animals not by looking at them superficially but by an appreciation and understanding of how their parts work together for the benefit of the organism.

But his lasting influence has come through his little work called *Poetics*, which was chiefly a discussion of drama, whether tragedy or comedy. One purpose Aristotle attributed to both tragedy and comedy was catharsis. This Greek word means nothing more than cleansing or purging, but what Aristotle meant by it is still debated up to the current day. He says that plays create a catharsis of pity and fear in the viewer. The traditional view has been that this is a purging of emotions from the audience, in the sense that negative emotions are disposed of, perhaps an analogy to medically purging impurities from the body.

Unlike Plato, Aristotle thought that mimesis was something positive and natural, a feature of knowing the world that we possess from childhood. In Aristotle's view, poetry is more philosophical than history, and part of this owes to the nature of mimesis. Aristotle's view of mimesis clashes with Plato on this point, for Aristotle thinks that the mimetic imitation of a play can in fact show the audience something of the philosophically universal, it is not merely an inferior copy of a copy.

Medieval Aesthetics

In the Middle Ages aesthetics was treated as a particular aspect of theology, as were many topics.

The view of beauty developed by Augustine seems to be in part a development of Aristotle's mathematical conception. Not only must something possess a kind of agreement between its various parts but it must also possess pleasing colouring. Ugliness is the absences of such qualities, at least to some degree because their lack is noticeable.

Augustine and others after him were keenly aware of their place as inheritors of a rich pagan tradition of art, and this interaction between pagan antiquity and the coming Christian Middle Ages produced interesting syntheses. For example, in the court of Charlemagne, the scholar and artist Alcuin of York (735–804 CE) made a very Platonic distinction between the appearance of beauty and eternal beauty. The appearance of beauty, taken correctly, only points us to eternal beauty. One fascinating application of this distinction was the difference Alcuin made between the visually oriented culture of the pagans and the Christian culture he himself envisioned. This mapped on to a difference

Alcuin of York.

between the Christian scriptures, which do not depend on sight but on contemplation, and the visual arts, perhaps indicative of pagan idolatry.

Thomas Aquinas added to theological philosophizing about the beautiful by equating it to the good. His suggestion was that they differ only in aspect, and beauty is the aspect of the good particular to seeing and hearing. He makes this point by observing that we say there are beautiful sights and sounds, but not beautiful tastes and smells. On his understanding, sight and sound aid the intelligence in a way that smell and touch do not. Aquinas' definition of the good is that it is that which everyone seeks, and thus there is an inborn human desire to seek the good, without which our desire will never be quieted. Evidently then, on Aquinas' view, seeing the beautiful is able to satisfy this intellectualized desire to see the good. So what is beautiful is good, but it is also true that the beautiful is rational, since it satisfies the intellectual need to see the good under the aspect of beauty.

Aquinas had three conditions for beauty he relates in *Summa Theologicae*. To be beautiful, there must be a completion or wholeness. There must also be a proportion. And lastly there must be a quality of brightness, clarity or bright colour.

Aquinas' Conditions for Beauty
A) Completion or wholeness
B) Proportion
C) Brightness, clarity or bright colour

Francis Hutcheson

Moving on to the time of the Enlightenment, Hutcheson has had a direct effect upon the trajectory of aesthetics in the modern sense. He wrote a work in 1725 called *An Inquiry Concerning Beauty, Order, Harmony, Design*, in which he divides the investigation of beauty into two elements: beauty as it relates to the person perceiving and beauty as it inheres in an object which is perceived. His emphasis on the internalization of the appreciation of beauty has placed him in the eyes of many as the founder of modern aesthetics. We have an internal sense of beauty on the one hand, and on the other it is the 'uniformity amidst variety' which grants to an object the beauty it possesses.

Francis Hutcheson.

There is a reason that Hutcheson attributes our aesthetic appreciation to an 'internal sense'. What he means is that it is almost as if we have a sense organ devoted to perceiving beauty, but unlike the others, this sense organ is inside and not on the outside of the body. An indication that this is the case, he argues, is that our awareness of beauty comes to us in the same way as a perception. Just as when we hear a sound, our ears immediately discern the pitch, loudness and quality of the sound, so our beauty sense immediately picks up on whether something is beautiful or not. He also points out that, just as our physical senses do not need to appeal to any principles, rational framework or logic to determine what they are seeing, this is also the case with our beauty sense. We do not need any theory or formalized laws to determine whether something is beautiful. We just see it.

HUTCHESON'S SENSE OF BEAUTY

JUST AS WHEN WE LOOK AT A CAR WE ACKNOWLEDGE
IT AS A CAR, SO LOOKING AT SOMETHING BEAUTIFUL
IMMEDIATELY STRIKES US AS BEAUTIFUL

A second insight Hutcheson offered was another reason why our sense of beauty must be internal and cannot be external. For this he offered the example of Isaac Newton's gravitional theorem, undoubtedly beautiful. The theorem is not something that is seen, at least with the eyes. It is comprehended by the mind, and this indicates to Hutcheson that the sense of beauty must be internal.

Hutcheson's other main pillar of his theory of beauty, concerning 'uniformity amidst variety' now needs some attention. Another way of putting this is that in objects of beauty there is both multiplicity and simplicity, or that something beautiful is both one and many at the same time. However, this is not to say that any arrangement of singularity and complexity results in beauty. Hutcheson promoted the idea that order or arrangement is what unites the two features of uniformity and variety. What is uniform contains variety within itself, and the complex order which it can manifest is what comprises beauty.

Immanuel Kant

Kant set forth his aesthetic theory in the *Critique of the Power of Judgement*. In this work he introduces four 'moments' – quality, quantity, relation and mode – which elaborate this theory. These are categories imported from his *Critique of Pure Reason*.

The first of these moments, quality, concerns the judgement that something is deemed beautiful or not beautiful. Kant says that this process is 'disinterested'. What he means by disinterest is that we make our aesthetic judgements without any appeal to the benefit we may derive from them other than the contemplative pleasure itself. The pleasure of beauty satisfies us by being what it is rather than offering us or bribing us with something.

Quantity is the second moment. The idea here is something we all can relate to, the independent nature of the object of beauty. Kant said that the beauty in a beautiful object is not something that I arbitrarily designate as beautiful. If something is beautiful, it is beautiful for all times, places and people, because the beautiful thing itself calls forth this kind of reaction to its beauty. Beauty is objective. It does not depend on you or me, and the disinterestedness of the first moment of quality plays into the second moment. The fact that something appears beautiful to us if it promises nothing from its beauty besides our enjoyment of the pleasure of contemplating its nature is, Kant says, evidence that beauty is universal, since it does not cater to individual circumstances.

Kant's Aesthetic

Quality: Deeming something beautiful or not.
Quantity: The beauty of an object is objective.
Relation: Form or design of the object of beauty.
Mode: Necessary satisfaction in the object of beauty.

The third moment is that of relation, and it concerns the content of what is perceived as beautiful. The precise object of beauty is the form of the object, considered as a design with spatial and temporal features. Yet it is also important that as we experience the beauty of the object we do not conceive of the purpose of the beauty as existing beyond the experience of the beauty itself. That is, the purpose of the beauty does not serve a practical end, nor is it made simply to cater to the particular interests of the viewer.

Mode is the fourth and final moment in Kant's aesthetic. In this moment Kant says that what is beautiful confers a necessary satisfaction. As human beings we all have the ability of having aesthetic taste, a sense that is shared but also subjective. Since it is shared, all humans can be expected to have common ground in their appreciation of the beautiful, while at the same time beauty promotes a subjective element of satisfaction. Kant says this satisfaction ought to be present, even if in some people it is not.

Important Principles of Aesthetics

The Diversity of Art

As we discuss various and wide-ranging aspects of aesthetic principles, it must be admitted from the start that what can be said in one area might not apply in another. If aesthetics chiefly concerns what is visual, and the different visual aspects of various arts differ drastically – from painting, exclusively visual, to music, exclusively non-visual – then it hardly makes sense that a given principle or even a theory can apply to all forms of art. What can be said aesthetically of the sculpture of an animal might not even apply to the animal that the sculpture is based on. Think of an ugly animal, perhaps a pig, which is used as the model for a sculpture that turns out beautiful. Our aesthetic judgement of the pig differs widely according to whether it is an animal or a sculpture, even though admittedly they are very similar objects visually. So it is very important that we carry an awareness of relevant aesthetic differences into our judgements.

DOES ART MAKE THE UGLY BEAUTIFUL?

AN UGLY, MUDDY PIG   A MOSAIC OF A PIG.

What Is Art?

In all our discussion so far we have assumed that there is such a thing as art and that we can experience it, and this itself is an assumption we can identify. Some of the theories of art, such as we will talk about below, work with an understanding of art already in place and seek rather to explain why art is appealing rather than what it is. But the question of what art is seems central to the philosophy of art, for in resolving the nature of what art is, we also understand how art can be created, what an artist is, and how to discriminate good art from bad art.

Yet the definition of art is not easy. This is in part due to the breadth of the term 'art' – applying to everything from written to visual and aural practices, from opera to graffiti to sculpture – and in part from the evaluative terms we often confer on art, such as good, bad, high or low. The concept 'art' must cover many different kinds of things and activities. Consequently, it is hard to distil what these disparate items have in common. This is even more true the further history progresses, with more schools and varieties of art being added all the time. Perhaps this is even the reason why our idea of art is hard to articulate, since our innate sense of what art can be is always one step ahead, eluding our conscious appreciation.

The term art can apply to everything from opera to classical sculpture to modern graffiti.

Wittgensteinian Art

One attempt to clarify the term 'art' was to concede that it does not have a strict definition, but rather admits of a variety of applications. This position has been formally named as a Wittgensteinian conception of art. Ludwig Wittgenstein introduced the concept of family resemblances, which could be applied to philosophical terms or definitions. Philosophers of art have applied this idea to art as well. Instead of having one focal shared meaning, different works of art share resemblances with each other. However, this does not mean that each work shares a similarity with each other work.

The idea of the Wittgensteinian theory of art is that there are varying degrees of overlap, similar to the overlap of some but not all features within a family. The mother and son have the same nose, but different chins, while the son and daughter have the same eyes as the father. No single feature is shared by all, but a great variety are shared throughout. Thus art is an 'open concept' which can be expanded by the group of artists themselves. One way of expressing this model of art is that art itself is artistic: it is constantly being reworked, altered and added to as an expansion of what art is.

THE FAMILY RESEMBLANCE OF ART

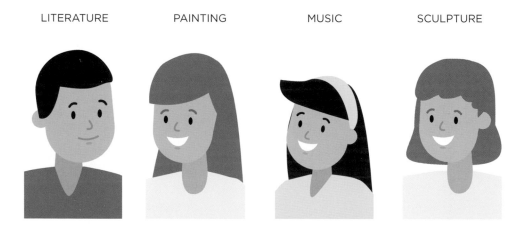

LITERATURE   PAINTING   MUSIC   SCULPTURE

SOME TRAITS ARE SHARED, BUT NOT ALL

This theory provides an important insight into the nature of art. It is obvious that, whatever else art is, it is an activity that involves creativity, often to such a degree that we consider the culmination of creativity to be the same thing as art. Some philosophers have seized on this feature of art and applied it to the Wittgensteinian theory, coming to the conclusion that since art is creative, and creativity involves developing new approaches and works, art is fundamentally something that creates novelty. This is to acknowledge that the definition of art, in a sense, is something that is always changing, because its frontiers are always expanding.

Positionality in Art

Most people, even if they engage in the production of art at some point in their life, are not artists. Most of us are art appreciators or enjoyers, but not artists, much less are we artistic critics, if we conceive that in a formal, academic sense. But yet all three – artist, audience and critic – inform our view of art. It is important to distinguish these different roles as we think about the nature of art and aesthetic experience.

On one extreme, art is the product of an otherworldly inspiration, and it is not fully understood, not even by the artist. If this is an accurate depiction of the artistic process then perhaps it is just impossible to dissect art. It must simply be appreciated as an inexplicable feature of human life, like love.

On the other extreme, from the perspective of the critic, art is something to be rationally analysed, and this philosophical process may even be necessary to properly enjoy or understand art from the perspective of the audience.

In between these extremes is the average experience of someone who enjoys art. They are not acquainted with the first-person experience of creating art, at least not at the high level of a professional or skilled artist, nor do they put much weight on the theoretical distinctions discussed in this chapter. For them, art is something they appreciate in the moment, and the beauty they see in art is a delight quite distinct from the experience of the artist and critic.

Beauty

Beauty is a term so associated with art that art could be deemed the science of beauty, or the activity of creating the beautiful. Of course the definition of beauty is as difficult as that of art. Plato was the first philosopher to suggest that there is one kind of beauty, 'beauty itself', from which all other kinds of beauty derive their name and kind. Regardless of whether beauty is one or many, the goal of art historically appears to be the production of beauty.

This view of art has changed, or at least apparently so, in the 20th century. Roger Scruton has argued that the motivating force behind contemporary art is a kind of desecration of the beautiful, while others have made the point that the horrors of 20th-century wars have affected our view of beauty in art.

This changing relationship to art suggests that our concept of beauty resides in us, or in some relationship we have to objects of art or beauty. Our concept of beauty could be nothing more than either the pleasure we feel or the judgement we make that something is beautiful. The source of the pleasure we feel in viewing art is quite mysterious when we consider the phenomenon. It often arises without any rational reflection on the work of art. We receive the pleasure as we perceive the beauty, in the same way that a hand perceives the warmth of a fireplace and simultaneously enjoys the pleasure of being warmed by that fire.

Participatory Perception

We began this chapter by noting that the word 'aesthetic' derives from the Greek word for sense perception. Whatever else art involves, it certainly involves perceiving an artistic object. But what is there about this activity that can help us in our understanding of art? We should begin with acknowledging that when we

Roger Scruton.

view art we enter into a different mindset or experience. We do not experience strolling through the Louvre in the same way as walking down the aisle of the local supermarket. Some might even say that the reason we create and enjoy art is in order to cultivate this special experience. If this is true, then the motivation for artists is to create works of art that especially provoke this aesthetic experience in viewers as a kind of participation. The crucial feature of this understanding of art is not only the fact that art possesses this unique aesthetic experience, but that audiences seek it out and artists intentionally incorporate this perspective in their art.

Ethics and Arts

At first glance, ethics has nothing to do with art. How could the study of the beautiful impact in any way on right and wrong behaviour? However, contemporary debates, especially about what is shown on film and television, indicate that there is a strong link between art and ethical considerations. This dispute can be traced at least as far back as Plato, who in his Republic banished the poets for corrupting the morals of the city, especially those of impressionable youth.

There are three main views often used in discussing the relation between art and

Art is an experience: these two walks are not at all the same.

ethics. The first is autonomism, a position that art is an independent enterprise and either cannot or should not be submitted to ethical considerations. One motivation for this viewpoint is that it just seems to be the case that some works of art are very good even though they are morally repellent in one way or another.

ART AND ETHICS		
AUTONOMISM	**MORALISM**	**IMMORALISM**
NO RELATION BETWEEN ART AND ETHICS	GOOD ART IS ART WHICH IS ETHICAL	GOOD ART IS ART WHICH IS UNETHICAL

Moralism can be taken as the opposite view to autonomism. According to some versions of this position, a work of art is flawed, or perhaps is itself immoral, if it has a moral flaw within it, and this moral flaw is somehow praised or elevated. Works of art have a didactic role in teaching us through their depictions. If teaching is an important and necessary element of art, then it is very possible that what they are teaching us concerns the way we live. This is nothing more than ethics, and so a movie, for example, which depicts and so teaches wicked things, is itself a bad movie. Importantly, it is a bad movie artistically *because* it is bad on ethical grounds.

A third view is called immoralism or sometimes contextualism. On this view, artistic works can possess aesthetic and artistic value for the very reason that they are immoral. There are various circumstances in which this can come about. However, a

A play featuring a killer: is this play unethical?

general principle is that there is a distinction between what is represented and what is endorsed. A particular character in a play may be a serial killer, but this representation can be redeemed in the larger viewing experience of the whole play, which portrays the killer in an unflattering way. Another situation in which this theory seems to have some merit is, for example, a movie which is attempting to change or undermine the predominant beliefs of an audience for the better. Imagine the audience possesses an unhealthy prejudice and the movie undermines this belief with a sympathetic character who is a target for such prejudice. Although the movie is transgressive, it effects this transgression for the betterment of the audience.

Representation and Expression

Earlier we saw that, at least since Plato, the predominant view of art has been that it is, or ought to be, representational. This is a view that says art tries to take objects in the world and depict or present them again, but in a changed manner. The painting of the flower is designed to 'represent' the real flower. The art mimics the original through interpretation, and to the degree it succeeds in doing so, it is good art.

It was inevitable that some rejected this view of art, and the expression theory, which looks less to the objects of art and more to its subjects, has been one of the most

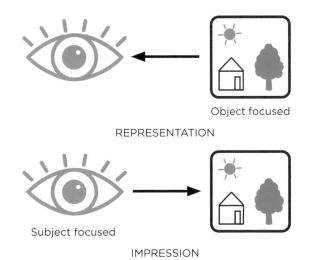

IMPRESSION VS REPRESENTATION

Object focused

REPRESENTATION

Subject focused

IMPRESSION

impassioned objections. This inward turn to the human side of art involves registering our subjective reactions to it, while at the same time relieving the artist of any obligation to make their art conform to the likeness of an original, as with the representational theory of art. If anything, the emotions and experience of the human artist take centre stage instead of the objects of art. It is this emotional capture of the artist that is transferred to the viewer. One way to mark the distinction is to say that what is represented is not the sunset as it appears but the *experience* of seeing the sunset as it appears.

The skill and mystery of art according to the expressionist view is being able to communicate these emotional experiences through media that are not emotions themselves but are emotionally invested. So the book or film or painting conveys to an audience sympathy or disgust or awe – for instance through a painting of a couple walking together in the rain or a film about a battle in World War II. The mere expressing of an emotion is not, however, art, as this might suggest. Two other elements must be present. Firstly, the artist must have some type of medium in which the art is expressed, it cannot suffice to go over to someone's shoulder and begin crying on it – this is not art, even though a strong emotion is conveyed. A further condition is that the artist must be intending to make art, and this includes something of the idea that a particular artistic work aims for an artistic effect of one kind or another.

Formalism

It is an indisputable point that art has a structure of some kind, and this we can term its form. The form is most evident in visual media, such as sculpture, painting or film, but it is also present in other art, such as the composition of music or the writing style of a novel. At any rate, with this theory of art, design looms large.

Primarily form is to be contrasted with the content or subject matter of the art in question. In some extreme versions of this position, there is *nothing* else that

We do not know who Mona Lisa was, when or where she lived, or even if she existed, to appreciate the painting.

matters except the form. A good example of this formalist commitment is the *Mona Lisa*. Looking at the mysterious intrigue which the painting possesses, one could easily grant that knowledge of who the woman is introduces an irrelevancy into the appreciation of the painting. To appreciate the painting itself we need only *look and see* the formal appearance. It is not even important whether Leonardo da Vinci had anything special in mind when he produced the work or even, in fact, whether Mona Lisa ever existed as a real woman.

However, just as with the expressionist view of art, formalism is at least partly a reaction against the representational theory of art. The key to understanding how formalism is not the same as representationalism is that there can be works of art with a formal structure which is not representational. For example, there can be a painting with a geometric configuration of different colourful shapes beautifully arranged, perhaps like you would see when peering through a kaleidoscope. This type of art is not intended to represent anything, but nevertheless the aesthetic value of the art is achieved because of a relation of the formal aspects of the painting.

Geometric art like this does not necessarily have to represent anything to have an aesthetic value..

As you may have guessed, this theory of art is good at explaining the appeal of modern art, which tends towards abstraction while using the advantage of formal composition.

Neoformalism

A more moderate stance of formalism, able to accommodate the central insight from this theory, is to acknowledge that while the content of an artwork is not everything, it is something. It might even be the case that the content of art is its single most important feature. Proponents of neoformalism have not overlooked this important aspect of art, and require art to possess both form and content. The relation between form and content, however, still remains somewhat difficult to determine. The neoformalist conception of art requires form and content in some relation, but the exact relation is hard to express as a formula. So one must be satisfied with saying something like content and form must be related 'appropriately' or 'in the right way' where, perhaps frustratingly, art is known only when it is seen.

The idea of formalism, and so neoformalism as well, has often been expressed as analogous to a container and the content of that container. Take a pudding bowl, which must be non-porous, so as to prevent leaking, and neither too large nor too small, to hold the pudding. In this sense the container limits and serves to shape the content of what is held within. Similarly, the form is a 'container' for the 'contained' of the content.

Functionalism

If the formalist theory of art looks at all the external aspects of a work of art, then the functionalist account can be said to focus in on those external features which are most important. By the functionalist account there is an assumption that a work of art has some overriding aim or purpose that is communicated. Once this purpose is acknowledged, we can then ask what features of the work accomplish the purpose and how they work together. The purpose need not be anything profound or subversive.

The American architect Louis Sullivan was a proponent of the functionalist slogan 'Form follows function'. This pithy insight tells us something else important about functionalism. It's not that functionalism denies there is a form, or claims form should be ignored; rather the idea is that the function of something should determine its form. In the case of architecture this will be something palpable such as the use of the building or the plot of land available, whereas in something like painting it will involve the more abstract aim of, for example, invoking awe or pity, or inspiration.

The old Chicago Stock Exchange building, designed by Louis Sullivan, a proponent of functionalism.

Aesthetic theory can help lead us to a greater appreciation of art.

Perception and Subjectivity

If a painting is painted in the woods and no one sees it, is it really a work of art? Art, as perhaps the most painstakingly deliberate construction of the human mind, naturally gives rise to the belief that what we see or hear when we turn our attention to the work of art is not something that is in us, but is in the work of art itself and we are privileged to merely *detect* it. For how else, one may wonder, would it even be possible for art to be appreciated as the work of an artist if what the artist made cannot be appreciated on the artist's own terms?

To frame this question in a different way, two ideas in particular might help in determining how much of art is subjective and how much objective. The first is that art cannot be merely reduced to measurements and parameters. Whatever it is, it is something that alights over and above a measuring tape and a magnifying glass. So it would be somewhat foolish to think that we could reduce art to something objective, as objects and artefacts completely independent of human observation. On the other hand, it is equally folly to think that art is entirely subjective, for to take but one property of one art form, colour, we have a quasi-objective property. Apart from the colour-blind, those who can see do see more or less the same kinds of colours. Their sight converges on an objective property of the art, and this can be measured to a degree. So art seems to be something neither entirely subjective nor entirely objective, but between these two extremes beauty dwells.

Principles of Aesthetics and You

When it comes to beauty and art, much as the field of art itself is always growing, so too our conceptual understanding of beauty and art is always expanding. Whether such scrutiny will deliver better art or at least different forms of art is very difficult to determine. So much of aesthetic thinking concerns getting our head around art that already exists. Applying theory to as yet non-existing art is perhaps beyond the scope of philosophy.

In a general sense, what aesthetic theory can offer is a greater appreciation of art than we possess without it. It can enrich art by revealing to us elements which were invisible to us before. Even though art lies open before us as something to look at, this does not mean that we 'see' everything that is there. But with the additional analytic tools of philosophy we can multiply beauty without taking any away. In doing so we increase the possibilities of discussing art with others, informing and being informed in different ways.

SUMMARY POINTS

- The Platonic conception of art involves mimesis: art concerns inferior imitation of originals found beyond the physical world.
- Aristotle's idea of beauty, unlike Plato's, centred on making beauty reside in the particular objects of beauty.
- Thomas Aquinas said the beautiful is that aspect of the good which involves seeing and hearing.
- Francis Hutcheson made a distinction between the beauty in the perceiver and that in the object.
- Taking a Wittgensteinian approach, art is not a term that has one essential definition, but rather some features of one work or field of art share some (but not all) features with others, just like the physical features of a family.
- Aesthetic experience is different in kind from experiencing a stroll through a store or walking through the different rooms in a house.
- Representationalism is the theory of art that says that art tries to imitate, to some degree, another object, natural or not.
- Expressionism is the theory of art which focuses on the internal subjective experience of art.
- Formalism focuses on the design or form of a work of art, neglecting the content or history of the work.

Chapter 9

THE PRINCIPLES OF POLITICS

The question of what we do as individuals is necessarily connected to what we do as a group. In ancient Greece the relationship between individuals and the community was understood in the context of the city-state, or *polis*. It is from the word polis that the art of *politike*, the political, comes about. So the political is a very broad term, encompassing everything that affects community life, corporately and down to the individual level.

We often associate politics strictly with the activities of politicians, but this chapter will deal with the political as a practical concern affecting people, laws, governmental form, customs, social agreements, ethics and much more.

Questions

What is the best form of government? What are the obligations of a government? What are the limitations of government and where does government gain its authority? What are the guiding philosophical principles that underlie political thinking?

History of Philosophy of Politics

Plato

The best articulation of Plato's thoughts on political thinking occurs in his work the *Republic*. The ostensible topic of the book as a whole is a search for the meaning of justice. In a dialogue to that end, Plato has the character Socrates voice a defence of the intrinsic worth of justice: someone should be just without any regard for the benefits it confers or whether actions will be discovered by others or not. Socrates' inquiry takes a curious route, for he thinks that justice in the individual is too small to properly investigate, so he decides to turn to justice in the city to see it writ large. This will give us a knowledge of justice in the city.

Plato's division of the soul, discussed in Chapter 7, relates directly to the political division of an ideal human society. Plato divides the city into three parts: the guardians, the auxiliaries and the craftsmen. The guardians correspond to the rational, the auxiliaries to the spirited, and the craftsmen to the appetitive part of the soul. The city fares well when the wisdom of the ruling class of the guardians is enacted by both guardians and auxiliaries for the benefit of the whole city. The auxiliaries, being the spirited element in the city, are soldiers, while the craftsmen perform the mundane manual labour necessary for the functioning of the city.

Some of Plato's policies in this hypothetical city are extremely controversial and provocative, such as the abolition of the nuclear family to promote solidarity among the citizens (on the grounds that ignorance about who one's parents are results in the assumption that all citizens are brothers and sisters). It is clear that Plato's aim is to organize the city for the betterment of the city as a whole. In the dialogue, the principle

PLATO'S CITY-SOUL ANALOGY

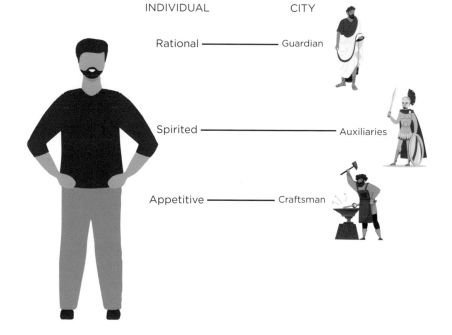

INDIVIDUAL   CITY

Rational ———— Guardian

Spirited ———— Auxiliaries

Appetitive ———— Craftsman

which organizes the city into the three classes is the idea that people must specialize in a certain role, and are adapted by nature to their special role. One unique consequence of this specialization is that the ideal polis should be ruled by a philosopher-king, someone with the knowledge of the highest philosophy who willingly steps away from this intellectual activity for the benefit of the city.

Aristotle

Aristotle wrote his own treatise, *Politics*, often directly engaging Plato on some disagreement. Aristotle thought, in contrast to Plato, that the art of politics was something distinct from the knowledge of the philosopher. The motivation for founding any city is different from a mere household or village. The household of the nuclear family is necessary for living. The village, which is a grouping of several of these families for mutual aid, is a furtherance of this same desire to promote life. However, it proves inadequate, because there is still a desire to live well, and this is where the polis comes in. The polis alone adequately provides for living well. Thus one Aristotelian idea is that the political is that which concerns humans coming together to live well, since this is the aim of the polis. The city, in other words, is the fullest manifestation of what is found at the household and village. All three levels – household,

ARISTOTLE'S POLITICAL DEVELOPMENT

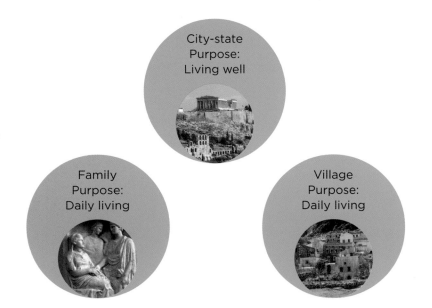

City-state
Purpose:
Living well

Family
Purpose:
Daily living

Village
Purpose:
Daily living

village and city – aim at the same object. For this reason Aristotle called politics the architectonic art, or the most authoritative. By this he means that all the other arts and sciences, such as laws, military planning and literature, fall under the scope of the political, for the political art decides to what purpose to direct everything else.

Cicero

In Cicero's political writing we see a sophisticated text informed by Plato, Aristotle and the Stoics. His most influential work was *De Officiis*, usually translated as *On Duties*. This book discusses human nature, the honourable, justice, magnanimity and propriety, as well as the possible conflicts that arise from these different virtues.

For Cicero, justice is the highest of the virtues and it is only by following this that a man can become good. There are two aspects to justice. The first is that no one should harm another unless he has been injured. In one colourful passage, later adapted by Machiavelli, Cicero notes that injury can come about in two different ways: by force or by fraud. Force is like a lion who overpowers the victim and rends them apart. But fraud is the worse injury, and is a like a fox.

The second element of justice is that public property is for public use and private property is for private use. What he means is that, although no private property is natural

– it must be won in war or inherited, for example – we must be content with the land that has come into our possession.

Injustice he also divides into two different kinds: the injustices of commission, where injury is committed against an innocent person, and those of omission, where someone fails to step in and prevent an injury of commission.

Cicero.

Thomas Aquinas

Political philosophy developed further during the Middle Ages. Aquinas is more famous for his theology and philosophy, but he also engages in political theorizing in different works. The most significant of his contributions perhaps concerns natural law and the form of government. Aquinas believed that there was a natural moral order to the world in general, and in the political life of men in particular. The aim of political life, laws and the form of government was to ensure a people conformed to the natural law. It is clear that Aquinas believed the clearest route to this end was rule by

Aquinas believed that kings could ensure people followed the natural moral law of the world..

a king. In a monarchy, a single set of eyes could envision the good for all and set about bringing this goal to fruition. This mirrors on an earthly level the governing structure of the divine realm. Like later thinkers, Aquinas does recognize that there are excesses and temptations associated with the power of a king. For this reason and perhaps others, he advocates a kind of mixed form of government. In one passage of the *Summa Theologiae* (also known as *Summa Theologica*) he says that, although the best form of government is rule by a single person, this is not managed alone, for there must be subordinate rulers. Surprisingly there are even democratic elements in the political system he advocates, such as that every ruler is chosen by all, and all people are eligible to be the ruler.

Niccolò Machiavelli

To be 'Machiavellian' is to garner no good reputation in contemporary usage. The label is associated with pernicious manipulation and unscrupulous motivation. But what did Machiavelli actually teach?

Machiavelli (1469–1527) lived in the Italian city-state of Florence during turbulent times. His vocation as a public servant came only after the Medici family were deposed, and when they returned to power Machiavelli was tortured for his assumed role in opposing the dominant clan. It was after this politically tumultuous period that he wrote his works.

One reason that Machiavelli has continued to draw new and interested readers is that he specifically offers advice to rulers. Since he mentions he is trying to draw attention to his present lowly status in the preface to *The Prince*, it is not beyond consideration that Machiavelli has his own promotion in mind, and that this appeal to rulers was a bid to improve his own status.

On another, more political level, however, the existence of hardship or misfortune serves as an important step in political rule. Machiavelli offers up four examples of rulers in legend or history whose wretched circumstances provided the conditions under which they transformed their communities. Theseus, the mythical founder of Athens, for example, had to overcome many trials of combat with ferocious man-like creatures such as Procrustes and the Pine-bender, and then upon coming to Athens, was recognized by Medea, who tried to have him killed. Moses, the leader of the Hebrews, had his difficulties in leaving Egypt and then had to wander for decades in the wilderness. Cyrus, the great historical ruler of the ancient Persians, initially had to labour under the thumb of overlords, the Medes. Romulus, the mythical founder of Rome, nearly died from exposure at birth and had to struggle with his brother for ascendency. The Machiavellian approach to these figures is to regard them as exemplifications of the idea that hard circumstances lead to opportunity. As some have said about contemporary politics, in a neo-Machiavellian voice, 'Never let a good crisis go to waste.'

Niccolò Machiavelli.

MACHIAVELLI'S EXEMPLARS		
EXEMPLAR	**STRUGGLE**	**ACCOMPLISHMENT**
ROMULUS	LEFT EXPOSED AT BIRTH, STRUGGLE WITH REMUS	FOUNDED ROME
CYRUS THE GREAT	SUBDUED BY MEDES	CONQUERED MOST OF THE NEAR EAST
THESEUS	FIGHTS WITH MANY MONSTROUS CREATURES	FOUNDED ATHENS
MOSES	WAS A SLAVE, WANDERED FOR 40 YEARS	FREED HEBREWS; REFOUNDED ISRAEL

Machiavelli's relationship to Christianity appears to be mostly negative. He criticizes the corruption of church leaders and pinpoints the influence of the pope as an obstacle to a unified Italy. Furthermore the role that he ascribes to fortune also seems to personify it into a force independent of the sovereignty of God. He praises the risk involved in pursuing fortune. On a more general level, Machiavelli compares his contemporaries unfavourably with figures from the ancient pagan past, who were unrestrained by various ecclesial shackles, leading a life of strength and boldness.

In Machiavelli's conception, one must not look to idealized and unrealizable political theories, but instead to the way that affairs actually work. The needs and health of the state are elevated above everything else, including individual freedoms and even conventional understandings of morality. Thus Machiavelli is focused on the ends, and the means are indeed justified by whatever ends promote the wellness of the state. In fact, virtue is measured by the degree to which it accomplishes this political aim.

Thomas Hobbes

Hobbes lived in a time of great national strife during the English Civil War. His *Leviathan* (1651) can be understood in light of this experience, since his political theorizing, at least in this context, begins from the realization that without the structure of government, men will descend into a wicked war of all against all. This is the germ of the idea that, in its natural state, life is 'solitary, poore, nasty, brutish and short'.

We can see that in Hobbes' conception of political organization there is considerable pessimism about human life. He believed that we are constantly in a state of unease as we are always seeking after something new. For many this results in seeking power, and since power is a finite commodity, this will necessarily lead to competition and, in extreme cases, violence and bloodshed. The supporting facts which Hobbes adds to his case are that humans are never so much stronger or weaker than each other as to make a difference in this struggle for survival. The strongest person is always vulnerable to the weakest, for example through poisoning or an ambush where thirty weak men take out five. So even if humans are not motivated by the accumulation of power (though many are), they will be forced through fear or prudence to accumulate power to defend themselves. Hobbes terms this the 'right of nature'. This right of nature leads, ultimately, to an unsatisfiable escalation: the possibilities of self-

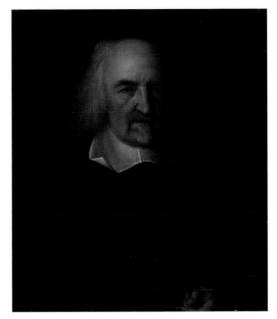

Thomas Hobbes.

defence can always reasonably be imagined to come at any time and take a wide variety of forms. Hobbes believed that, at a general level, this right of nature was evident in kings and the suspicious self-interest with which they treated other kings.

HOBBES' STATE OF NATURE	
A	**B**
MOST POWERFUL MAN	LEAST POWERFUL MAN
WISEST MAN	LEAST WISE MAN

Someone from column B is always a threat to kill anyone in column A, by poison, assassination, ambush, or joining forces with others.

From his own experience with the English Civil War, Hobbes believed that the unrestrained violence of that war was evidence of this right of nature as well. As a practical remedy to the drastic requirements of the law of nature, Hobbes says that we should adopt a law which very much resembles the golden rule 'Whatsoever you require that others should do to you, that do ye to them'. This can also be formulated in a negative way, such that you do not do unto others whatever you do not wish done to yourself. All of this

The Battle of Naseby in the English Civil War.

serves to make room for the introduction of the state. People, when they recognize the dangers of violence that come with living in a society, willingly set aside some of their rights in order to receive protection from a sovereign or other form of government. The power that this sovereign holds needs to be absolute, for it intervenes not only in decisions of war, but also in more mundane aspects such as law and taxation.

John Locke

Throughout the history of political philosophy to this point, especially in the West, theological presuppositions exerted an abiding influence on theory, seen in authors from Plato to Aquinas. In the 17th century, however, John Locke did much to moderate such religious concerns and to shift us more toward the contemporary system of secular rule.

At the centre of Locke's philosophy was a conception of freedom and rights. Locke considered the main purpose of a political system to be respecting the rights of others, especially in relation to their person and their property. He played up the importance of property to such a degree that many consider property rights to be the only rights truly recognized under his system. Owning property, however, is not so much what creates rights as what indicates rights. A person who owns little does not have fewer rights than someone who owns more, nor does someone who owns nothing have no rights. Rather Locke's idea is closer to the conception that human beings are property-possessors and owning things is a natural right. The aim of a political society is to prevent incursion on life, health, liberty and possessions and, to put it positively, to affirm these things.

Locke based his understanding of the political on a broad and non-sectarian theological grounding. The backbone of political compliance is the belief that the laws reflect the thoughts of a single legislator. This legislator is not only the source of the laws but he

John Locke.

creates them with the intent that they be followed. In the case of the human legislator, this is quite easy, given the explicit nature of laws, but in the case of God, the intention of the Creator is much more difficult to discern. What we are left with, in Locke's analysis, is what God has revealed to us through the nature he instilled in human beings. We have an inborn nature that we are to study and understand, a nature that is rational and confers rights since it necessarily dwells in many different people in a community.

In a group of rational and moral agents such as humans, the aim of each individual is to 'seek happiness and avoid misery'. This model takes it for granted that different people seek to satisfy their need for happiness in different ways, according to their aims and abilities, and accommodates this difference by allowing for political freedom to act in whatever way best allows them to achieve it. Closely related to the pursuit of happiness is the need for self-preservation, which Locke also grants as a right. So, for Locke, individual rights means not only that each person has rights, but that each has rights as an individual so that they can pursue the path in life that seems best for them. This conception of rights does not obligate us to further the happiness, or even the pursuit of happiness, of others, since that might deflect energy or passion away from our own happiness. What Locke does suggest is that we have an obligation not to hinder others and others have the obligation not to hinder our attempts at happiness.

It should be no surprise that one of the results of Locke's philosophy is that we should respect each person's religious conviction as an element of their pursuit of happiness. This not only leaves religious judgement to individual choice but also divorces the coercive power of the state from religious questions.

Jean-Jacques Rousseau

Another in the list of early modern philosophers who developed the concept of the social contract, Rousseau's theories were formed by his view of history and human nature. His political philosophy centres around the idea that human good consists in seeking, attaining and granting equality in a social context. This search for equality can also be described as a human need that seeks to be recognized and satisfied.

Rousseau disagreed with Aristotle that man is a political animal. Instead, he thought that in the original state of nature people would come together only occasionally, most significantly to procreate. Originally human beings were solitary, leading lives which they believed would benefit themselves as biological creatures, needing food, water and shelter. Recognizing this same impulse for survival in others, these primitive people would also attempt to help others in their struggle for survival, unless this sympathetic undertaking proved an obstacle to their own survival. After this aboriginal state of mankind, there is another condition, one which fundamentally changes the relationship humans have toward each other. As societies pop up through cooperative interests, sexual competition arises as a necessary element. There is a general atmosphere of comparison, both in comparing oneself to members of the same sex in competition with each other and in comparing members of the opposite sex to determine relative excellence. This leads to a complexity of socially mediated emotions and responses such as jealousy, love, desire and, in a general sense, acceptance and rejection.

This state does not last long, since societies develop past this initial state as they become more

Jean-Jacques Rousseau.

complex socially and technologically. As societies progress, there is an increase in strife and conflict. However, Rousseau is quick to point out that this is not as a result of the natural inclination of humans, but is a result of society.

Karl Marx

It would be impossible to go through the history of political thought without discussing the important contribution of Karl Marx (1818–1883). Marx believed that the universe is completely material, and this material basis for reality also has a very strong impact on political development and organization. In this political context, Marx identified what he called the means or forces of production. These means of production are the raw materials, machines, tools and factories which, when considered together as a whole and combined with human knowledge, produce economic goods and values.

The forces of productions give rise to a second level, often called the superstructure. This consists of norms, political structure, economic structure, culture and ideology. It is important to recognize that the superstructure and the forces of production are mutually reinforcing. On the one hand the forces of production give rise to the superstructure, and on the other hand the people in the superstructure naturally aim to stabilize the forces of production in whatever way they can.

POLITICAL STRUCTURE

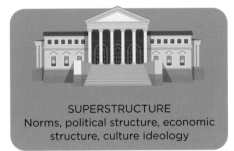

SUPERSTRUCTURE
Norms, political structure, economic
structure, culture ideology

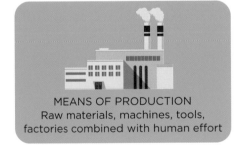

MEANS OF PRODUCTION
Raw materials, machines, tools,
factories combined with human effort

In Marx's analysis, there are various stages to history. The first is tribal, with the division of labour in society determined by the male/female distinction. Next is a slave society, in which the first manifestation of different classes appears, such as in ancient Egypt and Greece. Then feudal society emerges, with serfs providing their labour for agriculture. Lastly, a capitalist society comes into place when different forms of products and services can be exchanged.

Karl Marx.

Marx's political philosophy is marked by the prominent position it grants to class struggle. In a slave society, this is the clash between slaves and masters; in the feudal system, that between the serfs and lords; and in capitalism, the antagonistic relationship is between employers and employees. At some point in history, Marx predicts, the lower classes will seize power and true equality will result.

MARXIST CLASS STRUGGLE	
SOCIETY	**CLASS STRUGGLE**
TRIBAL	FEMALE AGAINST MALE
SLAVE	SLAVE AGAINST MASTER
FEUDAL	SERF AGAINST LORD
CAPITALIST	EMPLOYEE AGAINST EMPLOYER

John Rawls

Rawls was an influential 20th-century philosopher. In formulating his concept of justice, he was specifically aiming for an alternative to utilitarian and traditional approaches. He advocated an 'original position', designating not that this was an innovative contribution (though it was) but rather that it was a hypothetical condition of society we should

RAWLS' VEIL OF IGNORANCE

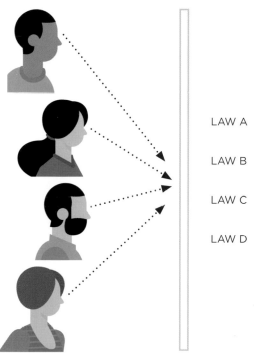

LAW A

LAW B

LAW C

LAW D

imagine from the 'position' of the 'origin' of a society. Rawls' conclusion was that we should adopt those principles of justice which everyone in this 'original position' would choose for themselves. We are to imagine a society enacted on the basis of a 'veil of ignorance'. That is, we are to suppose that we do not know the particular characteristics we possess – we could be a man or a woman, black or white, able-bodied or handicapped – and we are to assume that we do not know what our standing would be in society. Only by placing ourselves in this hypothetical position of ignorance are we able to operate from a position of impartial fairness.

John Rawls.

Important Principles of Politics

Equality

Equality is arguably the most appealed-to right and goal of modern political discourse. In this context, the extension of equality to historically marginalized groups is often the first thing that comes to mind. But what does equality amount to, and why is it valued so highly?

Perhaps the most obvious aspect is equality in a legal sense. The law affords equality to groups by recognizing that, for example, they have a right to marry. Granting a group which up to that point had not possessed the ability to marry this newly acquired right means that the group now possesses legal privileges and protections which it did

Gay marriage.

What determines the conditions for equality?

not possess before. We can imagine, and indeed it seems we even observe, that legal protection seems to confer a social legitimacy. That is, once the right to marriage is granted to a new group, the group becomes legitimized in the eyes of the society.

But at the heart of equality lies a moral status, and it is in virtue of being morally equal that equal treatment in society and under the law arises. The justification for this moral equality can take many forms. One is that it arises because of people's nature as rational agents, perhaps a view similar to Kant's, or because people ought to be treated as equal to oneself on the basis of self-interested reciprocity.

In some theories, equality is not an individual right, but is only valued at the level of society as a whole, such as in utilitarianism. Since, in this case, the measure of happiness is determined by the aggregate happiness of each individual in that society, then each person is equal in so far as their happiness is taken into consideration.

The grounds for determining equality are often to be illuminated by looking to those groups of persons who are disqualified from the protections of equality. Often this means those such as hardened criminals, children and the mentally insane. Such groups are excluded from full participation in equality for various reasons. At any rate, they show us that we do not think that merely being a person is sufficient to be granted equality.

The Idea of a Right

Closely related to the idea of equality is that of rights. In virtue of what do people possess rights, and who confers these rights? These are difficult questions, but clarifying the different kinds of rights is a first step in finding the answers.

Wesley Hohfeld, writing in the early 20th century, articulated a distinction of rights into four categories: claim, liberty, authority, immunity. In the following explanation, A possesses the right, B is the person whom the right affects, and X refers to the way in which the right is exercised. These will be clarified in the illustration. In a claim, A has a claim against B to do X. This also means that B has a duty to person A to do X. In the case of liberty, A has a liberty against B to X, while B has no claim against A to not-X. In an authority right, A has authority over B to do X, while B has a liability to A to do X. In an immunity right A has an immunity against B to do X, while B has no authority against B to not do X. These rights are relative to other humans, so that every right which is enjoyed comes about only in the context of other actions expected of other persons.

HOHFELDIAN ANALYSIS	
	EXAMPLE
CLAIM	MARSHA, AN EMPLOYEE, HAS A CLAIM-RIGHT AGAINST MITCH, HER EMPLOYER, TO BE PAID
LIBERTY	DAVID HAS A LIBERTY-RIGHT TO LIVE IN ANY CITY IN HIS COUNTRY
AUTHORITY	DOUG HAS THE AUTHORITY-RIGHT TO CHANGE, FORFEIT OR DELEGATE THE OWNERSHIP OF HIS HOUSE
IMMUNITY	MARSHA HOLDS THE IMMUNITY RIGHT AGAINST SOMEONE TAKING HER CAR. SHE IS IMMUNE TO THEIR CLAIM-RIGHT

The Family

Family has always been a focus of the political sphere. Plato thought that the city was simply a family expanded out even larger. In fact, he thought the best way to create unity within a city was for all the children to be unaware who their parents were, so that they would treat all males and females as siblings or parents, depending on their age.

The family sphere has also been important in that it has forged relationships which often parallel or are even thought foundational to political life. The relationships of husband with wife and parents with children introduce complicated issues for political life. Is it in the best interest of the state to promote families, and how can this best be accomplished? Do marriages have special rights which should be granted by the state, and likewise in the case of the parent–child relationship?

As for marriage, the state has to make certain decisions about what marriage is and how to regulate it. If it is for creating the next generation, then marriage will be regulated one way; if, on the other hand, marriage is whatever we choose to make of it, then there is little reason to apply various restrictions on who may enter into this arrangement.

Women and children come into the political equation as well. The rights of women historically have been tied to their role in the family and the degree to which motherhood and wifehood account for the political position of women. If women are subsumed into a larger goal in order to promote the traditional family, then their roles as mothers and wives will be afforded larger importance than as people with equal rights.

Children have often been of least consideration compared to the men and women in the family unit. There is a long tradition of treating children as belonging to parents, even if they are not, strictly speaking, property. This hints at perhaps the fundamental distinction between family life and the rest of political structure. The family is the centre of the private realm as marked out by contrast from the public realm, often understood as everything which is outside the life of the family. Rights of private property and privacy itself are necessarily tied into the family.

The family has always been an important unit in political life.

Liberty

Given that many modern societies participate in or aim at a liberal democracy (a democratic form of government under which individual rights are legally protected, from authorities as well as from other individuals), there arises a question about how we are to maximize the liberty implied in this concept. This is not only a question about what should be granted to the individual but also concerns what should *not* be granted to the powers of the state. In John Stuart Mill's case, he believed that power can only be legitimately wielded against people if harm is thereby prevented. This negative formulation of the scope of governmental power does not allow its coercive force to be deployed in the case of merely seeking the public good, for example, nor for advancing an individual's wealth or even virtue. This, in effect, is to grant the individual citizen tremendous power.

Mill believed that if people are granted unlimited power then this will lead necessarily to abuses of that power. The same caution should apply to governmental authority as well, so that the state only has the limited power to coercively stop harm against its citizens. Mill thought that the vast possibilities of beliefs, thoughts and actions that people can have, from prayer to public speech, do not harm others and therefore should not be prohibited or interfered with in any way by the government.

One important result of this view of liberty is that, although it applies to all, it most

MILL'S LIBERTY PRINCIPLE

THE STATE CAN ONLY INTERFERE TO PREVENT HARM, OTHERWISE
INDIVIDUALS HAVE A 'FORCEFIELD' AROUND THEIR PERSONS

CITIZEN A   CITIZEN B

CITIZEN C
Forfeits rights through
gun violence

conspicuously applies to those with unpopular opinions or behaviours. It is in allowing the most unsavoury and eccentric ideas and actions that this principle of liberty is truly put to the test. Mill is careful to also qualify his principle, in that the threat of harm can be a reason to forcibly stop someone in the right context, as well as harm itself. This becomes more difficult, as threats can easily be imagined or exaggerated.

Property

If liberty is one of the more important abstract concepts in political thought, then ownership of property is perhaps the most concrete example of a highly contentious topic. The main concerns regarding property in a political context are about whether individuals have a right to property and the way in which property should be doled out. Rousseau pointed out that land has been the occasion for many disputes, from simple violence to full-out war, merely on the basis of someone saying 'This is mine' while pointing at some tract of land they happened to come across.

LOCKE'S JUSTIFICATION OF LAND RIGHTS

OWNERSHIP OF LAND IS NECESSARY FOR SURVIVAL – FOOD, WATER, SHELTER, AND OTHER RAW GOODS

LABOUR MIXES INTO LAND AND TRANSFORMS IT, CREATING A BOND OF OWNERSHIP

What could be the justification for taking a piece of unowned land and transforming it into something that's owned, considering this as a question of justice or rights? One answer was given by John Locke. He said that land is necessary to the survival of people, and if no land was taken, people would die. This acknowledges that land provides water, food, shelter and the other raw goods necessary for human society. Locke also proposed that the essential action which justifies ownership of land is that someone contributes labour into the cultivation of that land. We can call this, in modern terms, 'sweat equity'. For example, if someone comes across unowned land and cultivates it, then the tilling, farming, clearing of brush, culling of animal life, gardening and any other activities performed upon the land mix the man's labour into the land. This gives him the right to own the land. We can say he has actualized the land, or perhaps completed it, in a way which would be impossible without him, and it is in possessing this 'livability' that the land is valuable to humans in the first place.

Toleration

This is a concept closely related to liberty and, in the modern context, to multicultural-ism. The contemporary understanding of 'tolerate' reflects the Latin origin of the term, 'to endure or suffer something'. It originally arose in the context of religious debates following the Protestant Reformation, but toleration can of course also apply in the realm of the personal, the political and countless other areas.

The idea of toleration is somewhat nebulously positioned between a positive and negative formulation. We positively grant something toleration when we refrain, for example, from sanctioning or criticizing it, but at the same time we usually hold a negative conception of the thing we tolerate – it is assumed we disapprove of or even hold in contempt that which we tolerate. It would be quite rude to tell someone in our acquaintance that we 'tolerate' them in our lives. The restraint at the heart of toleration marks out its oddity: toleration is not something we do, but something we do not do. This 'not-doing' is an action, in that it has significant consequences in many areas.

As mentioned, the historical occasion for 'toleration' as a word was the religious factionalism in evidence after the Protestant Reformation. Disputes among these factions were not sustained only in theoretical terms but spilled out into literal bloodshed. This, then, is the most important argument for toleration: that it prevents violence and death among competing views whose trajectory would often lead to irresolvable conflict.

The St Bartholomew's Day massacre, 1572, during the French Wars of Religion.

Reasons for toleration

1. Some convictions, especially religious and political, lead to violence.
2. Honours the sanctity of conscience and choice.
3. Toleration of Person A by Person B also involves toleration of Person B by Person A.

A second reason for toleration, especially in the formal, legal sense, is to allow for freedom of conscience and the pursuit of happiness. If a given religion, for example, is the only religion allowed, then all other religions are not tolerated. This compels in some way belief in a religion, which most people would grant violates their freedom, and moreover seems to enforce, even if a person changes religious beliefs, a coerced conformity rather than earnest adherence.

A third reason for toleration is an understood reciprocity among citizens. Citizen A might tolerate the unpopular political view of citizen B, but in turn citizen B tolerates citizen A's unpopular religious conviction. Grace is extended at least partially owing to the benefit that will be extended back in return.

Principles of Politics and You

The reach and significance of political theorizing is simply enormous, and affects us all in significant ways at all times. In the modern context, many citizens find themselves in the paradoxical position of living in the most free countries that have ever existed while at the same time taking up the monumental burden of shaping how one's own country is organized as a political state. This is not as simple as writing laws against theft and murder, but involves complicated philosophical reasoning about what situation we are in and in what direction we need to develop. Decisions include the role of rights, and which rights these are, the aims the government should have, the role which religion and morality play in society, and countless other issues. Political philosophy, of one kind or another, will inform our decisions about how we vote and what policies we advocate. It is not a question of whether we will have a political philosophy, but whether we will think out that philosophy clearly and consistently.

A well thought-out political philosophy is essential for determining how our society should be governed.

SUMMARY POINTS

- Plato's portrayal of justice in the *Republic* involves separating the city into three distinct classes.
- Aristotle said that political life involves living well rather than merely living or surviving.
- Thomas Aquinas thought the goal of political life is for people to conform to natural law.
- Niccolò Machiavelli offered practical political advice to rulers, defining virtue as the betterment of the state, not the traditional understanding of personal morality.
- In *Leviathan* Thomas Hobbes paints a picture of political life as something which is necessary, given the brutality of life without a government.
- Persons and their property are the chief concerns of political thought, according to John Locke.
- The human good in Jean-Jacques Rousseau's conception of a political society is to seek and attain equality in a social context.
- Karl Marx said that the material conditions of a society directly influence its economic and political structure.
- Wesley Hohfeld divided rights into four kinds: claim, liberty, authority and immunity.
- John Stuart Mill advocated a liberty principle that governmental power should only be wielded against people when harm is thereby prevented.

THE PRINCIPLES OF RELIGION

The philosophy of religion usually focuses on several issues: the persuasive force and logical character of arguments for the existence of God; the role of religion and morality; the never-ending dispute about the relationship between religion and science. There are, of course, many other areas involved in the philosophy of religion, but these in particular have captured most of the conversation and interest in recent decades.

Questions

Is there a God? Can we prove the existence of God? What do we mean by 'God'? How do we come to make religious decisions and have religious knowledge, if there is such a thing? What is the relationship between faith and reason?

History of Philosophy of Religion

The Hebrew bible declares, 'In the beginning was God...' and this assumption of the existence of God has long been a staple not only in religious but also in secular philosophy from the beginning of Western civilization. In ancient Greece, despite the contention over various metaphysical positions, there was one principle which all took as a starting point. This was the idea that nothing can come from nothing – the universe could not have arisen from something which was not there. For some philosophers, like Aristotle, this made them take the position that the universe was eternal, while for others it pushed them toward the idea that something or someone must have created the universe. With these examples from two different cultures, we can see that it is not always easy to distinguish religious from non-religious ideas. The Hebrews and Greeks both posited ideas consistent with the creation of the universe by one or more gods, though one appealed to revelation, the other to a fundamental belief that something that exists has to come from something else which already exists.

Socrates

Socrates is an interesting figure in the philosophy of religion, for he brings in an element of controversy when it comes to mixing philosophy and religion. Along with corrupting the youth, Socrates was charged with introducing new gods into Athenian society, and was put to death for having done so. His death demonstrates that religious questions are difficult to divorce from political, ethical and philosophical issues on any practical level. One abiding issue which was brought to the forefront during Socrates' trial and execution is the issue of life after death, which we will return to later.

In Plato's dialogue *Euthyphro*, the character Socrates embarks on a discussion about piety with the character Euthyphro, who has brought up a charge of murder against his father for killing a slave. Socrates tries to get to the core of what makes something beloved by the gods, since this is central to the idea of piety. Is a) what is pious pious because it is loved by the gods, or is it rather the case that b) what is pious is loved by the gods because it is pious?

The Death of Socrates *by Jacques-Louis David, painted in 1787.*

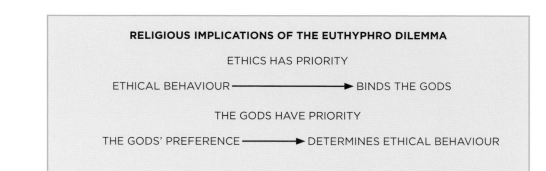

A skull rack from the Templo Mayor in Mexico City – if the Aztec gods advocated human sacrifice, did this make it pious?

On the surface the sentences by themselves are quite simple, but understood in relation to each other they form a profound paradox. The question centres around what makes the pious the pious – is the source in the gods or is it independent of them? If the pious is entirely dependent on the gods, then can the gods advocate whatever they want, say child sacrifice or cannibalism, and following the gods in this way would be pious? This seems like quite the counter-intuitive position, but the other option delivers an odd conclusion as well. If the determination of what is pious is independent of what the divine wills or thinks, then this means that the gods, not being the ultimate arbiters of what is pious, have something or someone over and above them.

Plato's dilemma is somewhat different from contemporary applications to monotheism, since in the dialogue an important detail is that there are multiple gods who can disagree among themselves as to the definition of the pious, something which cannot happen when there is a single god. Nevertheless, the Euthyphro dilemma continues to offer fascinating questions about the nature of the divine and its relationship to our world.

Epicurus

Epicureanism has long held a reputation as a philosophical system focused on the pursuit of pleasure. This is certainly true, but what most do not realize is that there are important religious assumptions that form the backdrop for Epicurean practice. Perhaps the key document in Epicureanism is the Principal Doctrines. It is a digest of maxims, the first two of which almost serve as preconditions for how to live out an Epicurean life of happiness: do not fear god and do not fear death. The gods, Epicurus says, are not concerned with what we do on earth, because they are in a state of utter happiness themselves. The fear of death, on the other hand, takes a little more work to overcome. When we exist, we don't have to worry about or much less be in the state of death, because we are alive. On the other hand, when we are dead, we simply aren't there – when death comes, we will never be there to greet it, we will be gone.

EPICURUS' ARGUMENT TO ELIMINATE THE FEAR OF DEATH

WHEN WE EXIST, DEATH DOES NOT.

WHEN DEATH EXISTS, WE DO NOT.

At any rate, dealing with the fear of death and with the worries attendant on pleasing the gods and avoiding their wrath by our mortal actions are two steps in achieving happiness on the Epicurean model.

Augustine

Saint Augustine, as he is widely known, is a figure whose contributions to both philosophy and theology were immense. Of particular interest, Augustine focuses on questions of knowledge and other aspects of the human mind. Starting as a young man in the exotic religion of Manichaeism, he grew disillusioned by its inability to answer hard questions. After becoming a Christian, Augustine used his classical rhetorical training along with a form of Platonism he had acquired through Latin translation to write works on the nature of language, scepticism, the nature of the will and psychological self-identity. In *The City of God* he sought to defend Christianity against the charge that it corrupted the Roman Republic. Among his many points is that pagan Rome had in it the seeds of its destruction well before the advent of Christianity, and that furthermore paganism itself causes many harms when evaluated in light of the eternity of the afterlife which is to come. Augustine makes the point that, while Christians live in the earthly realm, it is not their final home, since their highest loyalties belong to the spiritual realm with God. The city of men aims at the satisfaction of men and earthly ambition, to the neglect of God, while the city of God aims at the love and glory of God.

Saint Augustine.

Thomas Aquinas

Aquinas is probably the first person envisioned when the subject of philosophical theology or the philosophy of religion arises. He was equal parts theologian and philosopher – two professions whose aims and the talents required for their adequate employment do not always align – and it is fair to say, without in any way intending to impugn his fidelity to either camp, that Aquinas was equally committed to philosophy and theology in such a way that he sought to create a harmonious synthesis between the two fields. To some this has appeared to compromise one field in favour of the other. However, let's look at a few ways in which Aquinas sought to effect this synthesis.

From Aquinas' standpoint, philosophy and theology can talk about the same subject matter – they are not at odds and do not necessarily concern different topics – and this is because theology originates from God

Thomas Aquinas.

while philosophy often approaches the same subject matter but from the perspective of human reason.

When it comes to the good life, Aquinas' take on Aristotle shows how philosophy was often harmonized with Christian belief by alteration and addition. Aristotle taught that the life of happiness (*beatitudo* for Aquinas) was a complete earthly life lived in accordance with virtue. Of course, Aquinas believed in an afterlife, and if in fact there is an afterlife, our mortal life cannot tell the whole story of happiness: the ultimate happiness is to be found when the believer is united with God in the afterlife.

A fascinating application of Aristotelian metaphysics is found in the doctrine of the eucharist. The celebration of the eucharist is the Christian ritual of partaking in the 'body' and 'blood' of Christ through the memorial consumption of bread and wine. Aquinas' problem was that, although the bread and wine appear to be bread and wine, Catholic

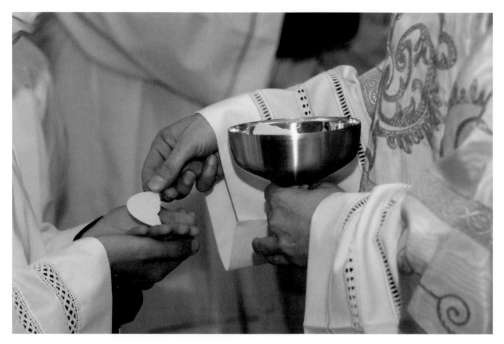

To explain the eucharist, Aquinas turned to Aristotle's idea of substances.

theology had traditionally taught that the bread and wine actually were Jesus' body and blood. To remedy this difficulty, Thomas appealed to Aristotle. Aristotle taught that there are substances, such as a horse or a person. If we take a horse as an example, the horse can undergo various changes, grow bigger or older, its hair can change colour through exposure to the sun, its mane can be trimmed, it can be trained as a racehorse or show horse, and so forth. Yet we take it for granted that, in the midst of all these changes, the horse remains the same horse. Aristotle said this is because the horse is a substance, while all the changes the horse undergoes are accidents. The substance is the essence of a thing which lies underneath its appearances. Applying this to the case of the eucharist, Aquinas said that while the accidents of the bread and wine are nothing more than bread and wine, the substance of the bread and wine is transformed into the body and blood of Jesus.

Søren Kierkegaard

By the 19th century, Kierkegaard was reaching brilliant theological insights which were unique and penetrating. Unlike, say, the rationalism of Aquinas, Kierkegaard believed that dedication to Christianity necessitated an open embrace of paradox and even absurdity. The central absurdity in Christianity is that the transcendent, eternal God was made a man in the person of Jesus Christ. There is inherently a logical stumbling block to the acceptance of the Christian life, which therefore cannot be accepted on the basis of rational decision. The choice of accepting Christ as God must instead focus on an assessment as to whether Christ as the divine is offensive or not. If it is offensive, then one has given up on the power of faith.

Choice itself looms large in Kierkegaard's philosophy (he was the originator of existentialism, which holds that one's every action constitutes a choice that shapes who one becomes), and it is the possibility of choice which causes anxiety. Choice is double-sided, for, while

Søren Kierkegaard.

it forecloses on the possibilities of life by making a determinate decision with certain consequences, it also confers a psychological delight at having partaken in the freedom of our own decision.

Whereas some religious systems act as a mere go-between for people and the divine, Kierkegaard rejects this kind of setup, since it fails to account for the burden of individual choice which must always be undertaken by oneself, not through others. Even though there is importance in each and every act of choice, there is a sense in which choice itself is never fully consummated. This is especially true in the context of faith, where the decision to live the life of faith must be constantly reaffirmed through the act of another decision. This repetition accounts for the constitution of the true self.

In Kierkegaard's analysis, there are three stages of life, which do not correspond to mere chronological development but rather to spiritual maturity. These are the aesthetic life, the ethical life and the religious life.

The aesthetic life is a life of perceptual interaction with the world. It concerns only the immediate and as a consequence can form no coherent plan for life because of unconcern for purpose or the future. A person's interests are so superficial that they cannot in any way be satisfied by them, and this results in their abandoning one thing and hopping along to something else.

The ethical life focuses on the inner self. Often this kind of life assumes the responsibility of marriage and children, and it involves at least a degree of order that the aesthetic life cannot deliver. Because it turns to the self, instead of external goods and experiences, the ethical life commits to developing abilities and is less concerned with success in some worldly sense.

STAGES ON LIFE'S WAY		
LIFE	**ACTIVITY**	**ORIENTATION**
AESTHETIC	IMMEDIATE PLEASURE, SHORT-TERM	OUTWARD
ETHICAL	MARRIAGE, FAMILY, MORTAL LIFE	INWARD
RELIGIOUS	LIVING IN LIGHT OF THE ETERNAL	GOD

The partaker of the religious life looks to God's will and submits their own will to it. Whereas the ethical man submits their life to reason and morality, the man of the religious life turns to God alone. The best example of this is Abraham, who listened to God who told him to sacrifice his son Isaac. What the religious life demands is that one live life in light of what is eternal, God and his kingdom. This requires a leap of faith for one to follow God and subordinate earthly aims and activities to this singularly important purpose.

Immanuel Kant

Kant was brought up in a Lutheran household, though his religious beliefs by no means remained unchanged in his mature philosophy. He believed that God, as the all-sufficient being, is responsible for the individual nature of things as well as their higher-level fit into a unified cosmos. Thus he preferred to emphasize the role that God plays in establishing necessity and possibility, as opposed to the traditional association of deity with the infinite. In Kant's assessment, divine will and intellect are not in tension, as some previous philosophers had suggested, but are in essential agreement with each other. The grounding of necessity and possibility are found in the person of God.

When it comes to the question of religious faith, Kant emphasizes the importance which religion contributes to moral life. For this reason he advocates a pure rational faith, which in Kantian terminology means conceding that there is a practical rather than an intellectual need for the existence of God.

Despite his focus on the character of God, Kant nevertheless does commit himself to the idea that fundamentally humans are incapable of knowing God. As part of his larger philosophical project, he posits that we cannot pierce through and get beyond the appearances of the physical realm before us. The conclusion of his line of thinking is that we cannot rationally arrive at the existence of God.

Kant aligns human moral life with the existence of God as a benevolent, all-powerful, good and all-knowing being. Happiness can only be attained through morality, and yet only a being who knows the proper arrangement of the world in order to realize such a complicated standard of happiness could bring such morality into being.

Important Principles of Religion

The Design Argument

Also called the teleological argument, the design argument includes the idea that the world was made for a purpose (Greek *telos*). Simply put, it makes the case that the universe gives evidence of having been designed, and this designer is no one else except God.

This argument itself is quite old, matching up with common human experience; many have thought, looking at the intricacies of animal life or the starry night sky, that a creator must be responsible for the complexity and beauty of the natural world. Plato, Aristotle and Cicero, among the ancients, made design arguments. The argument is derived by analogy.

A famous such example was given by the 18th-century theologian William Paley. In his book *Natural History*, Paley asks us to imagine we find a pocket watch sitting upon the ground. As opposed to a rock which we might come across, arousing no further thought, a pocket watch has to have been placed or dropped there at some time. We would be forced to imagine that there was a creator of the watch who had made it, and he or someone else had lost or placed the watch on the ground. The watch had to be designed; its existence could not be explained away by saying that it has always been there or that it came into being by itself. It is all the more foolish, Paley thinks, to say that the visible world, with all its variety, complexity and unified design, has not been created by a grand designer, identified with God.

Paley's watchmaker argument: the universe is much more complicated than a pocket watch, so both are designed by a creator.

The teleological argument: the design of the universe is evidence of a creator.

Perhaps the most potent objection to the design argument has been the theory of evolution as first proposed by Charles Darwin and later developed into a full-fledged scientific paradigm. Natural selection weeds out, by death, those organisms, behaviours or features of terrestrial life which do not confer an advantage in survival, so that only those organisms reproduce which have beneficial features. Thus there is no design or designer responsible for the complexity (at least of organic life); the hallmarks of design are merely appearances of design.

One attempt to revive the design argument has been 'intelligent design'. Intelligent design has several different features, and the general scope of the argument is meant to specifically counter the Darwinian argument that design in the biological realm is apparent rather than real.

Two ideas in particular demonstrate the focus of intelligent-design arguments. The first is irreducible complexity. This is the claim that the complex organization we see in animals, whether at the macro or at the microscopic level, displays such a level of interdependence that if one single element were to be removed, the organism or mechanism would simply fail to work.

In the context of Darwinian explanation, this means the animal or plant would die. The intelligent-design proponent says this shows that the animal is so sophisticated that the feature could not have developed gradually, over time, with each step being added through progressive evolution. Either the sophisticated visual organ of the eye was entirely in place, or there would be animals with eyes which are effectively blind, and since these animals would be eliminated through natural selection, the gradual march toward fully functional eyes would never get started. The second idea is specified complexity. 'Specified' means something like having a pattern of information it represents. This is a feature common to all design, say intelligent-design advocates, and so it serves as common ground to admit design in the biological realm as well.

Information can be specified. For instance, the first letter from the beginning of this sentence is 'f'. Taken by itself, and not as part of the word 'for', it is specified, but simple. However, something can also be complex without being specified, such as the string of nonsense letters 'agtye gyopl twqad'. This grouping of letters is not specified because it does not conform to some informational pattern, which in this case would be English words. The paragraph you are reading is both specified, because it conforms to information embedded in the form of letters, and complex, since many different letters and words make up the paragraph. Proponents of intelligent design would say that this paragraph shows evidence of intelligent design – even if the theory of intelligent design does not. But they furthermore would apply this to the world, which itself has specified complexity and so is designed.

DARWINIAN NATURAL SELECTION

TIME

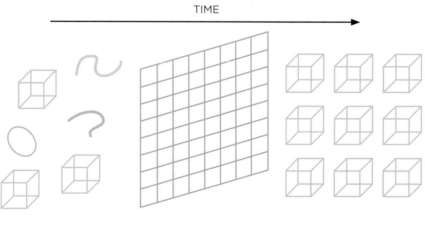

| A mixture of random shapes | A filter with square holes | The only shapes which can get through the filter are cubes, and cubes 'appear' designed. |

IRREDUCIBLE COMPLEXITY
ALL ELEMENTS OF THE MOUSETRAP – THE CATCH, SPRING, PLATFORM,
HAMMER, HOLD-DOWN BAR, AND BAIT – MUST BE PRESENT FOR IT TO WORK.
JUST LIKE A MOUSETRAP, LIFE COULD NOT DEVELOP GRADUALLY

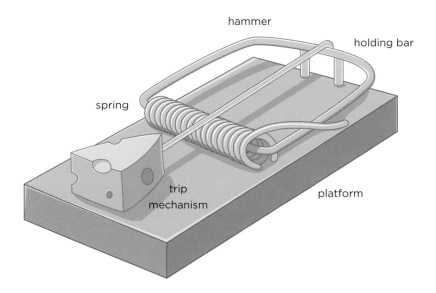

Cosmological Argument

This argument for the existence of God depends on the existence of the universe. Unlike the design argument, the cosmological argument does not point to any particular features of our world, but rather claims that the universe existing in the first place is evidence of God.

There are variations of the cosmological argument, but one of the most important features they share is an emphasis on contingency. Everything within the universe is passing away and decaying, and shows no evidence of being eternal and unchanging. This suggests the universe as a whole has originated from something or someone else. The universe was not, and then became. *Ex nihilo nihil fit* is the Latin expression of this idea, that nothing comes to be from nothing. If there is no existing thing, there can be no source or origin from which a subsequent thing can come to exist. By all appearances, the universe is something that came to exist, but it had to have come from something which itself already existed, and this is nothing other than God.

THE COSMOLOGICAL ARGUMENT

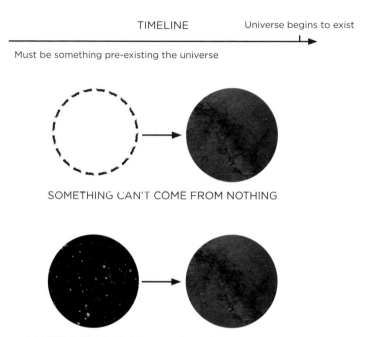

TIMELINE   Universe begins to exist

Must be something pre-existing the universe

SOMETHING CAN'T COME FROM NOTHING

SOMETHING MUST COME FROM SOMETHING ELSE

Another expression of this type of argument is the *kalam* cosmological argument (a name derived from medieval Islamic theology), which argues that whatever has a beginning of existence has a cause of existence. This would apply to the universe itself, since it began to exist. Thus there must be something responsible for the beginning of the existence of the universe, and this is God.

Ontological Argument

The most subtle and difficult of the arguments for God's existence, this has also pro-voked the most resistance, since it seems to work in a sophistical sleight of hand. The argument appeals to the essence or nature of who God is, and this is the 'ontological' part of the name, from the Greek word for 'being'.

A first version of this argument came from the 11th-century English theologian Anselm. The argument goes like this. We can conceive of that being than which no greater can be conceived. But to exist in reality is greater than existing only in the mind. It follows that, when we are conceiving of that being than which no greater can be conceived, we are thinking of a being who actually exists rather than one who exists only *in our imagination*. If we are thinking of a greatest being who has all the superlatives and capacities of goodness, omniscience, omnipotence, omnipresence, etc., and this being does not exist, then we are not in fact thinking of the greatest being. The reason is that we can conceive of this same being as existing, and that in fact is the greatest being, not one who only exists in the mind. The conclusion of the argument is that God exists.

Two famous objections to this argument have been made. One was made by Anselm's contemporary, Gaunilo, who said that he could conceive of the most perfect island, but that this does not entail that the most perfect island actually exists. Immanuel Kant, among others, said that existence is not a property, and so cannot be predicated of something the way colour, or height or age, among other things, could be. So nothing is added to the idea of a bed if we contrast a bed and a bed *that exists*.

The modern philosopher Alvin Plantinga came up with a variation and many think an improvement on Anselm's original ontological argument. Plantinga's version arose from his study of possible and necessary worlds. He says that it is possible there is a maximally great being. This means there exists a possible world with a maximally great being. But to be maximally great would involve existing in every possible world, since to fail to exist in every possible world would not be maximally great. This maximally great being existing in every possible world would include our world. So it turns out that God exists.

St Anselm.

Theodicy

Despite the exotic-looking word, 'theodicy' is the label affixed to a very common theological problem involving human experience: the relationship between a good God and the existence of evil. 'Theodicy' itself is derived from Greek and means 'legal charge [against] God'. The charge in question arises from the apparent inaction of God given the prevalence, or perhaps even the mere existence, of evil. If God possesses all power, all knowledge and all goodness (in other words is omnipotent, omniscient and omni-benevolent), the theodicy points out that these attributes are inconsistent with the existence of evil. For if God is completely good, but doesn't do anything about evil, then he doesn't possess all power to bring this about. On the other hand, if he does have the power to do away with evil and yet does nothing, then God is not good, for this would cause him to in fact eliminate evil. This is often framed as a dilemma between just these two options, but a third possibility is sometimes added, that God simply does not know about the evil going on all around us. The

Job rebuked by friends – one of the most famous examples of the theodicy dilemma.

conclusion is supposed to show that God does not exist, or at the very least, does not exist in the way we have typically assumed, since he is either not completely good, not powerful or not knowledgeable.

The most successful answers to the theodicy problem centre on free will. They suggest that the existence of moral evil in human life is due to the existence of free will, which God has provided to mankind as a necessary condition of being rational. Although the existence of free will makes evil possible, the overall benefit of free will is so great and so good that God permits the evil that it brings to exist as well.

Related to this idea is the defence that our own knowledge of evil is quite limited compared to the total knowledge which God possesses. So, the thinking goes, what appears to us in the present as an indefensible evil is, either in the long term or with all available information, actually something that is transformed into a good. It is like the pain a child undergoes in submitting to a needle, thinking that the pain is endured for no reason, when in reality the piercing pain was inflicted to inoculate the child. This is analogous to our limited knowledge of why God does what he does.

THEODICY

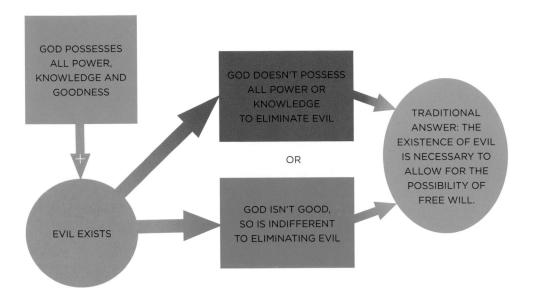

Religion, Science and Reason

Religion has often been contrasted with reason, and more recently, with the field of science. There is an implied incompatibility between the two areas of human life. To be religious, is, it is thought, incompatible with being rational; religious belief, in this view, is something like a blind leap into the abyss. But is there a necessary conflict between religion and reason?

There are reasons to believe that faith and reason can coexist. The first is that many intelligent people, including great philosophers from Plato to Augustine to Elizabeth Anscombe in the 20th century, have maintained religious convictions while also evidencing marvellously rational intellects. A second reason is that religion and reason are not opposites, so there is no justification for thinking they cannot exist at the same time. The opposite of religion is not reason, but irreligion or not possessing religious convictions. The opposite of reason is not religion, but irrationality, lacking rationality. And since reason is fundamentally different from religious belief, this means that their content is different, and so their jurisdiction simply concerns different types of things.

Perhaps religion concerns how we ought to live, while science and reason concern more mundane affairs. Some, like the palaeontologist Stephen J. Gould, have granted this division such significance that he coined the idea of 'non-overlapping magisteria'. According to this conception, religion and science have their own autonomous domains, where they may deliver pronouncements about ethics and physical facts respectively, but they cannot intrude upon the expertise or subject matter of the other field of human experience. Such a strict division may appear to follow a more pragmatic approach of political peace rather than reflect a fundamental division in reality.

Religious Experience

Religious belief is often justified or reinforced by religious experience. Are such experiences permissible as evidence for the existence of God, or for religious beliefs in a more general sense? Are they binding only on the person who has had them, or ought they carry some significance even for those who have not experienced them directly?

Perhaps the most common type of religious experience is that of conversion. Converting from a state of non-belief or from one religion to another involves a total involvement of the mind and spirit. It affects one emotionally as well as intellectually.

One mystery of such conversions is whether the conversion is the result of a prior change of mind, or if it is the very cause of the change of mind. Often these conversions lead to a dramatic shift in lifestyle as well as beliefs.

The aforementioned conversions need not involve any special otherworldly experience, such as the appearance of an angel or divine being, or manifestations of supernatural power. However, many religious experiences do involve a dramatic occasion when someone undergoes an ecstatic state, or is subject to revelatory visions or someone manifesting strange, apparently otherworldly behaviour, such as speaking in tongues or being given insight into the minds of others.

The philosopher and psychologist William James has enumerated four

William James.

different qualities in a mystical experience, generalizing across different religious traditions. 1) The experience is *ineffable*, difficult or impossible to capture in words. 2) The experience is *informative*: it grants knowledge one did not possess previously. 3) The experience is transient in that it does not last long. 4) The experience is *involuntary* since there is nothing that can be done to bring on or prolong the experience.

Miracles

The reality or even possibility of miracles has been a contentious topic in the philosophy of religion for millennia, for it involves the divine, nature, experience and the limitations of our knowledge. Even the very definition of miracles is something to be disputed. Consider a miracle to be something like an event that operates outside of the laws of nature. Working with this definition, a virgin mammal giving birth to offspring is a biological event which would strike many as an astonishing occurrence and for many an obvious miracle. Yet this process, known as parthenogenesis, has been observed to occur in the wild, by biologists no less. One possible conclusion we can generalize from this example is that any time anything occurs in this current universe, it cannot be considered a miracle. For if a miracle is only defined as something that occurs outside of the laws of nature, and some event X occurs in this universe, say a virgin koala giving birth, then it cannot be considered a miracle. Whatever happens is part of the course of nature, and on this understanding, an anomalous event is simply taken to be a new instance of a previously unknown phenomenon.

The previous discussion of miracles rules them out as a matter of definition: if something happens at all, it cannot be a miracle. But apart from this thorny issue of defining whether a miracle can happen, a miracle is supposed to be an intrusion of the divine realm into that of the mundane. Some take a miracle to be a sign of exactly this, an indication of the presence of God. Whether or not miracles occur, and whether or not it accurately captures what a miracle is about, this take on miracles does not require any violations of natural laws but treats them more like bells on a merchant's door which alert him to the presence of a customer; likewise a miracle alerts us to the presence of God.

Revelation

There are few religious images more familiar than Moses taking down the two tablets of law from Mt Sinai, handed him directly by God. Revelation, that is knowledge given from God to individuals or a people, is considered to be such an important feature that

Moses receives the tablets of the law.

religions are often described in terms of whether they are revelatory or not. A quick definition of revelation might be something like the miraculous communication of knowledge. Several elements are present in the idea of revelation and render its claims very potent. A god or gods have delivered the information in some fashion, so there is a mood of infallibility, since the source is divine. The recipient of the divine message is considered extremely important – after all it is this recipient, out of all people, with whom the divine has wished to communicate. The message itself, whatever its content, implicitly brings with it a measure of importance and perhaps requires our immediate attention. For these and other reasons, the message of revelation makes a claim on the audience to be accepted and to be believed.

As it turns out, and this is no insignificant point, revelation is always linguistic, and this in turn, in most cases, has lead to the message of the revelation being written down as a text. The study of the text in subsequent generations then takes on a tradition of its own, with different interpretive schools forming in an attempt to find the most faithful reading of the text.

Of course, one could readily reject, and many do, the message of revelation for many reasons. Scepticism about the veracity of the messenger and doubts about the content of the message, or even disbelief in the divine, number among the most common objections to divine revelation.

But even putting aside such worries and assuming revelation is true, there arises a certain difficulty in assessing how we are to take the message of revelation. If we assume it is infallible, what is the relationship between our interpretation of the message and its infallibility? Can we ever reach the true meaning of divine revelation?

Principles of Religion and You

Religion and religious thought have been with us for thousands of years of human history. Whether or not you yourself are religious, religious frameworks and assumptions are common throughout the world. Nor is there a clear distinction between religion and philosophy. Often these two fields inform one another in some way, enriching and

Religious thought is another lens through which to view the world and often overlaps with philosophy in its aims and methods.

strengthening or directing and focusing the subject under consideration. Understanding the historical way that philosophers have engaged with religion not only clarifies different ideas, but establishes common ground as to what is common between different religions and other systems of thought.

Many systematists, like Thomas Aquinas, have found an easy agreement between religion and philosophy, while others play up the differences between the two fields. Whatever your own take on their relationship, there is a striking amount of material common to both these two attempts to come to a fundamental understanding of reality.

SUMMARY POINTS

- The philosophy of religion has traditionally focused on the existence of God, and the relationship between science, ethics and religion.
- Thomas Aquinas advocated a life in accordance with virtue, just like Aristotle, but his formulation included an afterlife as well.
- Søren Kierkegaard wrote about three stages on life's way: aesthetic life, ethical life, religious life.
- Immanuel Kant did not think that the existence of God could be proved rationally.
- The design or teleological argument states that the complex design seen in the world requires a designer or creator, identified as God himself.
- Intelligent design says that the features of organisms demonstrate the design hallmarks of specified complexity and irreducible complexity.
- The cosmological argument for God's existence claims that something or someone needed to exist prior to the cosmos in order to explain it.
- The ontological argument for God's existence centres on conceiving of a being than which no greater can be conceived.
- Theodicy is the idea that God's omnipotence, benevolence and omniscience are incompatible with the existence of evil.
- William James captured four features of a religious experience: ineffable, informative, transient and involuntary.

SUGGESTED READING

The following list contains recommended reading material. It is a mixture, broken down by chapter, of both primary historical texts laying out philosophical positions for the first time, and of secondary materials reflecting on these historical texts. The secondary material will often be easier to understand and will provide a good framework before jumping into the complicated theories of someone like Immanuel Kant, for example. Due to space constraints, only a few books can be recommended under each chapter. So if the ideas in a particular chapter of this book pique your interest a good plan is to explore the topic further by studying one of the books below, often browsing through the secondary recommendation first and arranging further reading from there.

Chapter 1: Principles of Nature
Primary:
The First Philosophers by Robin Waterfield
Physics by Aristotle
Secondary:
Theory and Reality by Peter Godfrey-Smith

Chapter 2: Principles of Knowledge
Primary:
Book VI of *The Republic* by Plato
Meditations on First Philosophy by Rene Descartes
An Enquiry Concerning Human Understanding by David Hume
Critique of Pure Reason by Immanuel Kant
Secondary:
Epistemology: A Contemporary Introduction to the Theory of Knowledge by Robert Audi

Chapter 3: Principles of Metaphysics
Primary:
Phaedo by Plato
Metaphysics by Aristotle
Introduction to Being and Time by Martin Heidegger

Secondary:
Metaphysics: A Contemporary Introduction by Michael J. Loux and Thomas M. Crisp

Chapter 4: Principles of Logic
Primary:
Categories by Aristotle
A History of Formal Logic by I.M. Bochenski
Secondary:
Logic: An Introduction by Greg Restall

Chapter 5: Principles of Ethics
Primary:
Nicomachean Ethics by Aristotle
Theories of Ethics by Gordon Graham (contains both primary and secondary readings)
Secondary:
Ethics: A Contemporary Introduction by Harry J. Gensler

Chapter 6: Principles of Language
Primary:
Cratylus by Plato
Categories by Aristotle
Secondary:
Philosophy of Language by Alexander Miller

Chapter 7: Philosophy of Mind
Primary:
De Anima by Aristotle

Secondary:
Philosophy of Mind by Jaegwon Kim

Chapter 8: Philosophy of Aesthetics
Primary:
Poetics by Aristotle
Critique of Judgement by Immanuel Kany
The Birth of Tragedy by Friedrich Nietzsche
Secondary:
Philosophy of Art by Noël Carroll

Chapter 9: Philosophy of Politics
Primary:
The Republic by Plato
Politics by Aristotle
Leviathan by Thomas Hobbes
Secondary:
An Introduction to Political Philosophy by Jonathan Wolf

Chapter 10: Philosophy of Religion
Primary:
Euthyphro by Plato
Proslogion by St. Anselm
Faith and Rationality edited by Alvin Plantinga and Nicholas Wolterstorff
Secondary:
Introducing Philosophy of Religion by Chad Meister

INDEX

PICTURE CREDITS